AF407643

Dedicated to those who have not yet seen, in the confidence that what is intelligible will one day stand revealed.

COVER WORK OF ART:

Figueroa, William, Crucifixion Resurrection, 1999.
Collection, Private.

Revised edition, February 2026
First published December 2025
ISBN (paperback): 979-8-218-90281-0
ISBN (hardcover): 979-8-234-01806-9
ISBN (e-book): 979-8-234-02011-6
LCCN: 2026904530
Printed in USA

Author's Note

This volume is issued as an independent scholarly edition in order to make the work available in a stable, citable form. The manuscript's argument, structure, citations, and visual apparatus are complete; the present edition intentionally adopts a minimal production design so that the work may be read primarily as philosophy.

The illustrations included here function as perceptual demonstrations in support of the text. They are referenced internally and captioned for clarity. Where images are drawn from public-domain or Creative Commons sources, credits are supplied; where a diagram is original or adapted for explanatory purposes, it is indicated as such. Any permissions required for later production stage use may be addressed in a subsequent edition.

All rights to the text and original materials are retained by the author. This edition is published independently and is intended to remain compatible with future editorial review, revision, and reissue in collaboration with an academic or trade press.

William Figueroa
2025, December

The Light That Forms

Vibration, Meaning, and the Ontology of Appearance

Contents

Preface

Why This Book Begins with Phenomena Rather Than Theory

This book does not begin with definitions, arguments, or historical exegesis. It begins with phenomena.

This choice is deliberate. Contemporary discourse often treats ontology as something inferred after theory, or imposed through conceptual frameworks. As a result, explanation precedes observation, and form is too easily reduced to convention, projection, or mechanism. The aim of this book is to reverse that order—not polemically, but methodologically.

Before we ask what reality is, we must attend carefully to what appears.

Across disciplines that are normally kept separate—acoustics, optics, geometry, cognition, and aesthetics—one finds the same fact recurring: form arises from vibration. This recurrence is not interpretive. It is observable, repeatable, and lawful. Wherever oscillatory processes stabilize, ordered structures emerge. These structures are not imposed by mind, culture, or design; they arise as intrinsic articulations of the process itself.

The chapters that follow proceed from this fact.

Rather than beginning with metaphysical assertions, the book adopts a demonstration-first approach. Each early chapter focuses on phenomena that can be directly encountered: sound becoming visible, vibration organizing matter, geometry emerging without design. These demonstrations are not illustrations of a theory introduced in advance. They are the ground from which theory must arise if it is to remain accountable to reality.

Only after this groundwork is established does the book move toward ontology, semiotics, and aesthetics.

This ordering reflects a classical conception of philosophy. In ancient natural philosophy, metaphysical principles were not posited arbitrarily; they were articulated in response to order already encountered in the world. Harmony preceded number; form preceded definition; intelligibility preceded explanation. The present work stands within that tradition, though it speaks in a contemporary register.

Aesthetics plays a central role in this project. Not as ornament, and not as subjective preference, but as a domain in which intelligible structure becomes perceptible. Artists, designers, and attentive perceivers have long recognized that form carries meaning intrinsically—that shape, proportion, rhythm, and radiance are not neutral carriers awaiting interpretation, but expressive in themselves. This book takes that recognition seriously and treats aesthetic perception as a legitimate mode of access to ontological structure.

It should be stated clearly what this book does not attempt to do. It does not seek to replace empirical science, nor to compete with specialized disciplinary explanations. Nor does it advance mystical claims under the guise of philosophy. Its concern is more fundamental: to ask what must be true of reality if the same patterns of form, order, and intelligibility recur across domains that modern thought has learned to separate.

The argument, such as it is, unfolds by exposure rather than by deduction. The reader is invited first to see, then to recognize, and only later to name.

For this reason, metaphysical light, meaning, and ontology are introduced gradually. They are not premises, but conclusions drawn under necessity—once the phenomena have been allowed to speak.

The first three chapters therefore ask for a particular discipline of attention. They do not require agreement, but they do require patience. What appears there will determine everything that follows.

Part I — What Appears

Chapter 1
Form Appears From Vibration

Before theory, before explanation, before interpretation, there is a fact that presents itself repeatedly across domains: form appears from vibration.

This is not an inference, nor a metaphor. It is an observable condition.. Whenever a medium capable of response is set into oscillation, form emerges—not arbitrarily, not subjectively, but according to lawful patterns that stabilize, repeat, and reappear across radically different contexts. Order emerges as self-organizing structure. Form is not imposed upon vibration; it is what vibration becomes when coherent.[1]

This book begins here. Not with ontology, not with history, not with philosophical assertion, but with what appears.

When a surface is vibrated at specific frequencies, nodal structures emerge. Regions of relative rest and motion organize themselves into ordered patterns. These patterns are not added from outside, nor are they designed or symbolically imposed. They arise because vibration differentiates space.

The phenomenon is not confined to any single domain. Sound waves in air, oscillations on membranes, electromagnetic radiation, neural firing patterns, and even conceptual structures all exhibit this same property: oscillation produces organization.

Figure 1.1

Standing Wave and Interference Pattern

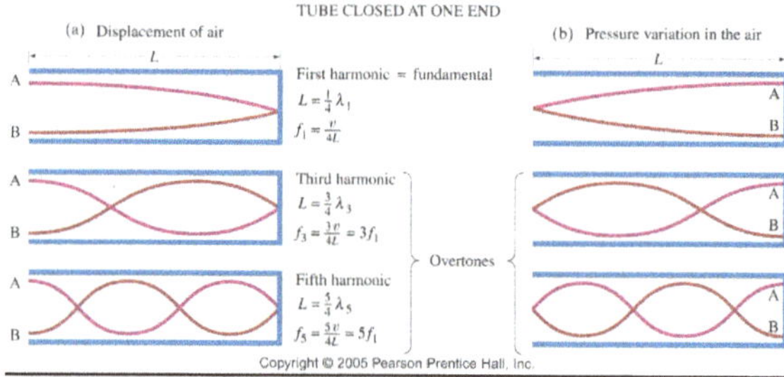

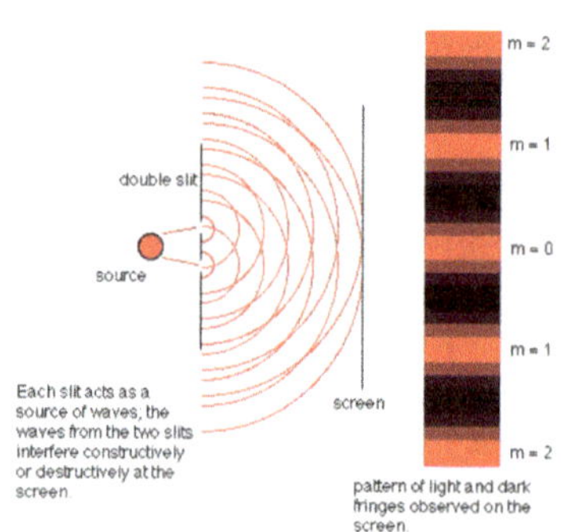

Standing wave and interference patterns demonstrating ordered structure arising from oscillatory motion

What matters here is not the material involved, but the process itself. Vibration is not a thing; it is an activity. And form is not imposed upon that activity—it is what the activity becomes when it stabilizes.

From Motion to Shape

When vibration enters a medium, the medium does not respond chaotically. It responds selectively. Certain configurations persist while others collapse. Over time, stable forms remain.

These forms are not decorative. They are solutions—ways in which energy, space, and constraint cohere.

Figure 1.2

Cymatic Pattern Formation

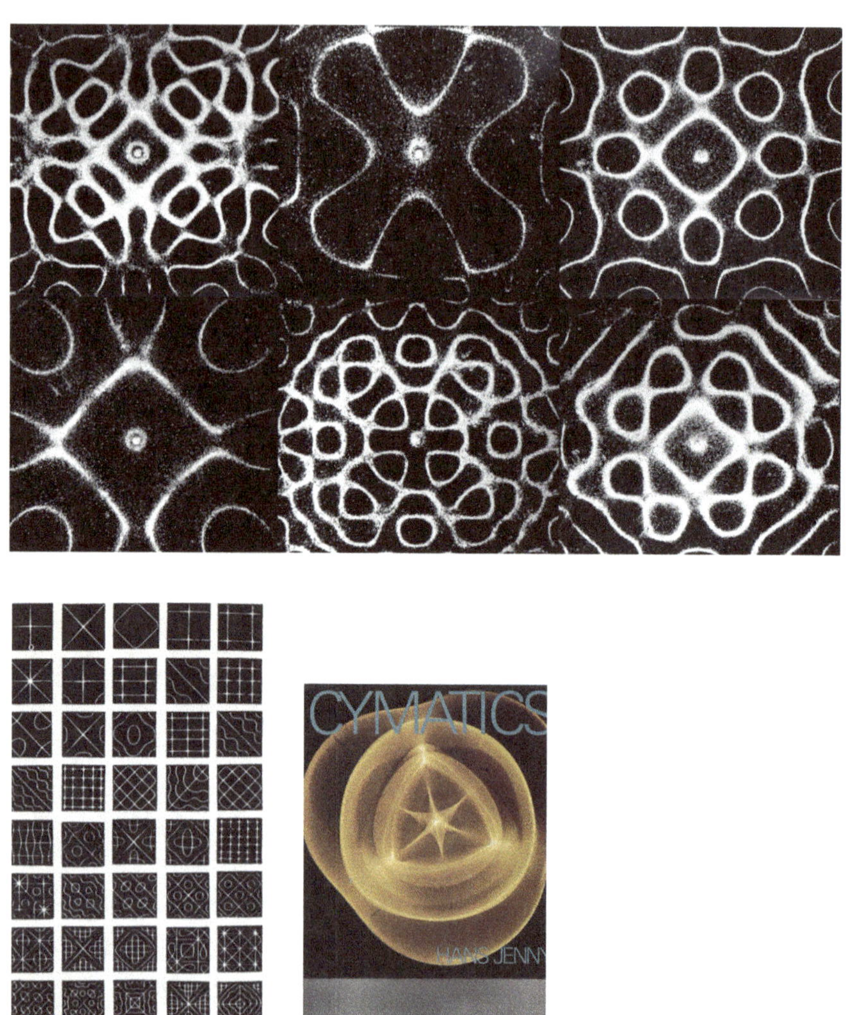

Cymatic patterns produced by sound-induced vibration in granular and fluid media.

In cymatic experiments, granular material or fluid organizes itself into distinct geometries when exposed to sound frequencies. Each frequency yields a different configuration, yet the configurations are never random. They are structured, symmetrical, and internally coherent.

The implication is immediate: form is not static matter; form is stabilized vibration.

This observation challenges a deeply ingrained assumption—that form is something added to matter. Instead, matter reveals itself as responsive, and form emerges as an event.

The Same Process Across Domains

What appears in these experiments does not remain local.

- In acoustics, vibration becomes harmonic structure.

- In optics, oscillation becomes wavelength and pattern.

- In neuroscience, rhythmic firing becomes perception and meaning.

- In geometry, stabilized ratios become proportion.

- In cognition, patterned activity becomes intelligible form.

The recurrence is not accidental. It suggests a unifying principle: vibration is the mode through which form comes into being.

At this stage, no metaphysical claim has yet been made. What has been established is empirical in the strictest sense: a phenomenon that appears repeatedly, lawfully, and across domains.

Yet repetition itself raises a question that cannot be avoided.

The Question That Emerges

If form arises everywhere through vibration, what accounts for the intelligibility of that process?

Why does vibration not merely dissipate?

Why does it organize?

Why does it yield structure rather than noise?

Physics can describe how vibration behaves, but description alone does not answer why vibration consistently yields intelligible order rather than arbitrary motion.

That question exceeds any single discipline. It belongs to ontology.[2]

What This Chapter Establishes

- Form appears wherever vibration stabilizes.
- This appearance is lawful, repeatable, and cross-domain.
- No appeal to symbolism or subjectivity is required.
- The phenomenon precedes explanation.

We have only observed—and what has been observed demands explanation.

Chapter 2
Sound Becoming Shape

Sound is the most direct and accessible instance in which vibration reveals its capacity to generate form. Unlike many physical processes whose structure must be inferred indirectly, sound makes its organizing power perceptible. It can be heard, measured, and— under the right conditions—seen.

Sound does not merely travel through space or stimulate sensation. Sound articulates space.

In Chladni experiments, particles migrate away from regions of maximal motion and settle along nodal lines—zones of relative stillness. The resulting geometric patterns correspond precisely to frequency.[3]

The sound differentiates the surface. Form appears as self-organization.

Resonance and Selectivity

Resonance is not amplification alone. It is a coherence condition. Where vibration aligns with a system's internal structure, form stabilizes.

Sound does not impose order—it reveals it.

Figure 2.1

Chladni Plate Pattern

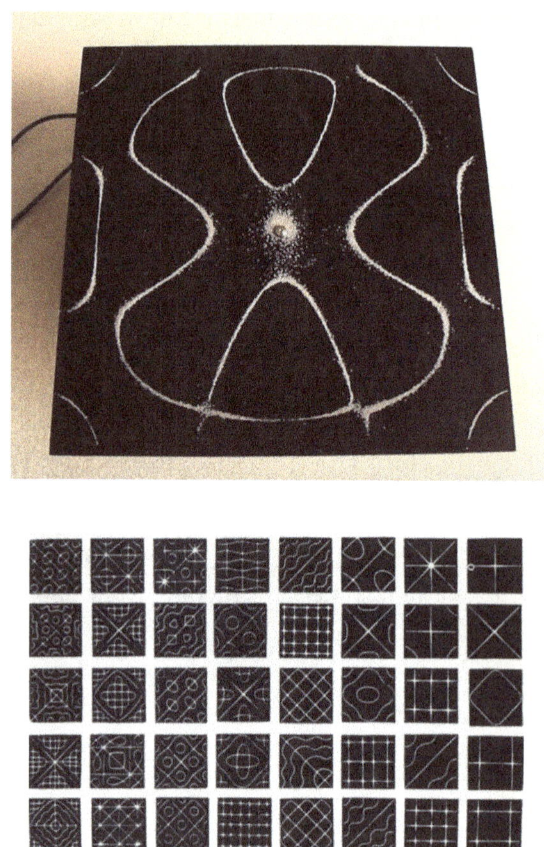

Granular material organizing into nodal patterns on a vibrating plate at discrete frequencies.

Figure 2.2

Cymatics in Fluids

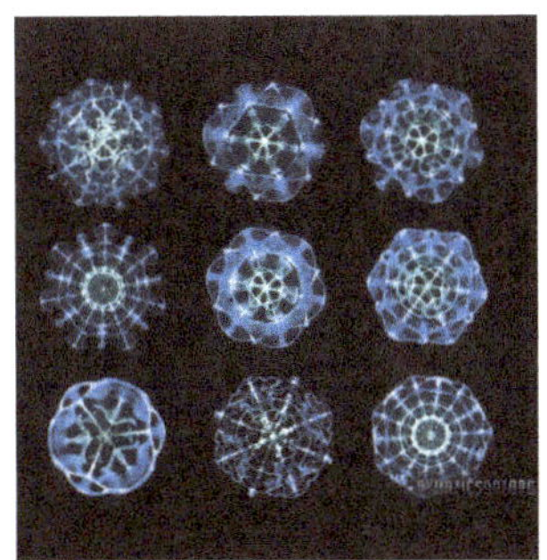

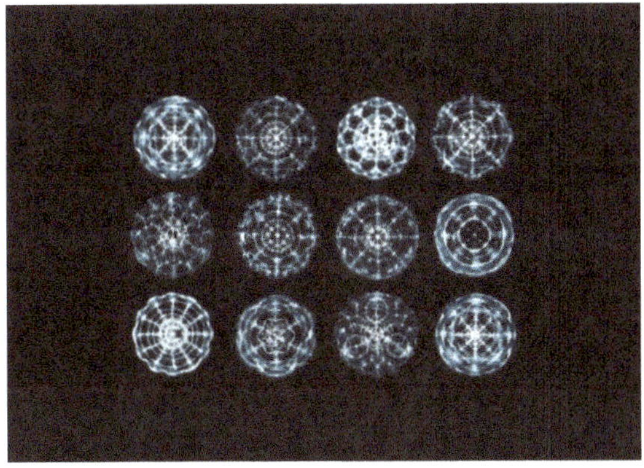

Fluid surfaces forming symmetric structures under sustained acoustic excitation.

In fluids, sound produces standing wave patterns that arise, persist, and dissolve with changing frequencies.[4] Form here is not object but event.

Sound demonstrates that temporal oscillation can yield spatial structure.[5]

From Time to Space

Sound unfolds in time, yet produces spatial form. Time leaves a trace in space. This transition is not metaphorical—it is physical.

What This Chapter Establishes

- Sound makes vibration visible.
- Vibration articulates spatial form.
- Geometry emerges without design.
- Order precedes interpretation

Chapter 3

Geometry Without Design

Geometry is often treated as abstract and imposed. Yet wherever vibration stabilizes, geometry appears—not as plan or projection, but as consequence.[6]

Figure 3.1

Symmetry in Natural Pattern Formation

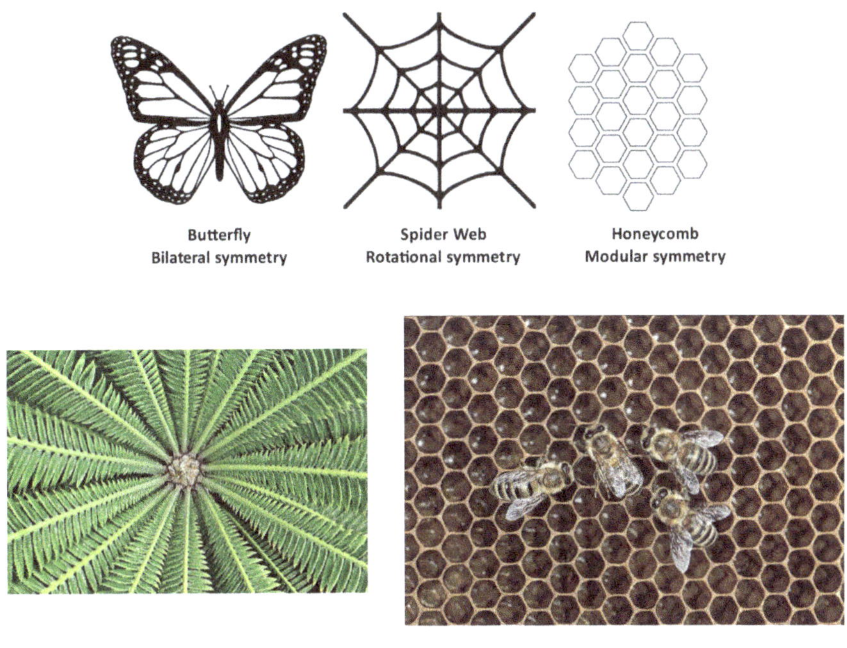

Recurring geometric symmetries appearing across natural systems.

Symmetry emerges where competing forces balance. Geometry is economical—it is what coherence looks like.

Proportion as Relation

Geometry expresses relation. Only certain proportions persist.[7] These are not conventions; they are ontological attractors.

Figure 3.2

Platonic Solids and Structural Stability

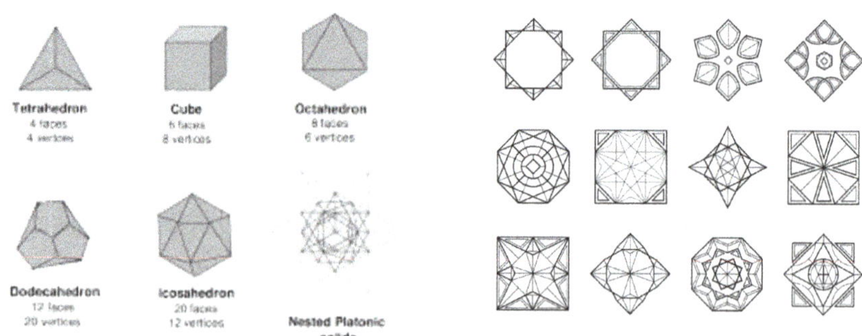

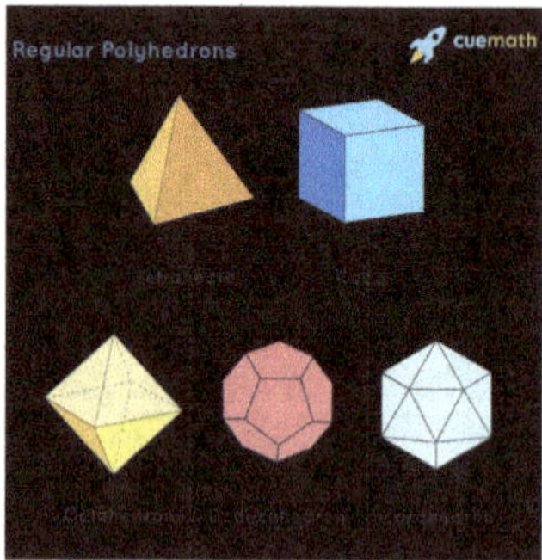

Platonic solids illustrating maximal symmetry and coherence.

These forms persist historically because they recur structurally wherever symmetry is maximized.[8]

Geometry as the Memory of Vibration

Geometry records where motion has achieved coherence. It is the trace of dynamic process, not static design.

What This Chapter Establishes

- Geometry emerges from vibration.

- Form is necessary, not arbitrary.

- Structure precedes meaning.

Transition to Part II

If form is intelligible by nature, then meaning cannot be purely conventional.

The next chapter introduces the principle that accounts for this intelligibility.

Part II - What Must Be True

Chapter 4
Light That Is Not Merely Physical

Up to this point, no metaphysical principle has been named. Form has been shown to arise from vibration; sound has made vibration visible; geometry has appeared as stabilized coherence. The demonstrations have been allowed to stand on their own.

Yet a question now presses with unavoidable force.

If vibration yields form, and form yields intelligible structure, what makes intelligibility possible at all?

Geometry is not merely structure. It is readable. Proportion is not merely efficient. It is meaningful. The order that appears is not blind regularity, but articulated coherence. At this point, explanation can no longer remain purely descriptive.[9]

Contemporary research on neural oscillations, coherence dynamics, and phase-locked activity offers empirical parallels to this claim, describing how intelligible patterns arise only when differentiation is constrained by coherence rather than randomness. These accounts do not explain intelligibility itself, but they describe conditions under which articulation becomes stable, readable, and ordered. In this sense, they stand as descriptive counterparts to the ontological distinction developed here.

What must be introduced is light—not merely as a physical phenomenon, but as a condition of intelligibility.

Physical Light and Its Limits

Physical light is well understood in scientific terms. It is electromagnetic radiation, characterized by wavelength and frequency, propagating through space and interacting with matter. It enables visibility by making surfaces perceptible. Without it, the visible world disappears.

But physical light alone does not explain why what is seen appears as ordered, coherent, or significant.

Light can illuminate chaos as easily as form. It reveals whatever is present, but it does not account for why what is present is intelligible. This distinction is decisive.

Physical light makes appearance possible, but it does not explain appearance as meaning. It is a necessary condition for perception, but not a sufficient one for intelligibility.

To explain intelligibility, another sense of light must be introduced

Figure 4.1

Electromagnetic Light and Perceptual Visibility

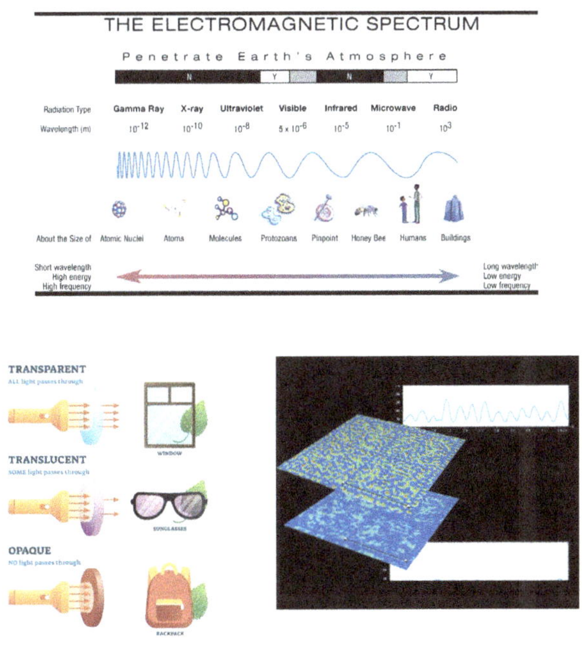

Physical light enabling visibility through reflection and illumination.

Light as the Condition of Intelligibility

Classical philosophy recognized a distinction that modern discourse often neglects: between light as a physical phenomenon and light as a metaphysical principle.[10]

Metaphysical light is not electromagnetic. It does not travel through space, does not have a wavelength, and cannot be detected by instruments. Yet it is no less real. It names the condition under which form is intelligible rather than merely present.[11]

This is the light in which order can appear as order.

Where physical light makes things visible, metaphysical light makes them understandable.

Figure 4.2

Light as Disclosure Rather Than Illumination

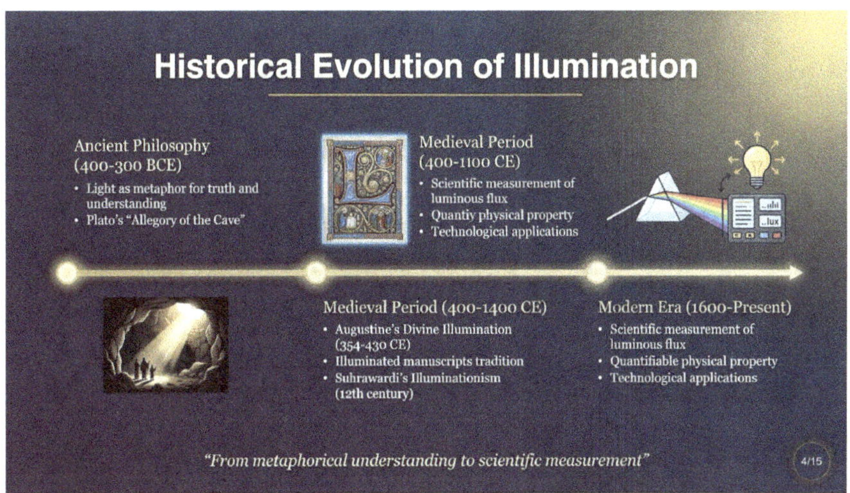

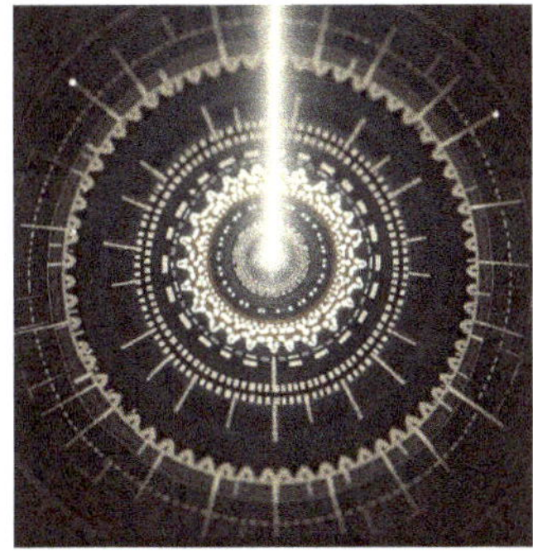

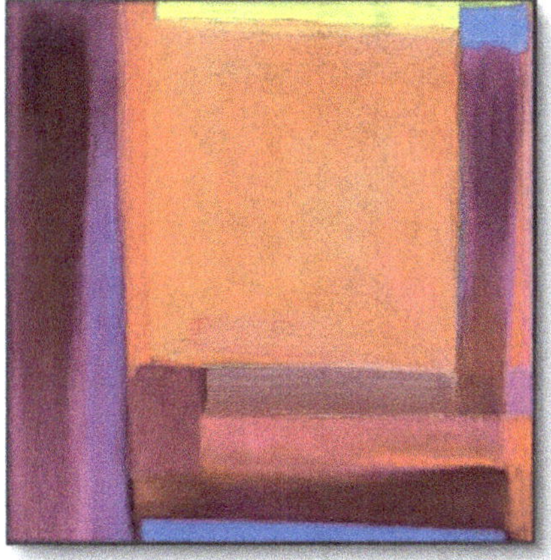

Light represented as disclosure of structure rather than physical illumination.

This distinction does not introduce dualism. It introduces levels of articulation.[12]

Physical light operates at the level of sensation.

Metaphysical light operates at the level of intelligibility.

The former reveals surfaces.

The latter reveals form.

Why Intelligibility Cannot Be an Afterthought

One might attempt to explain intelligibility as a projection of the mind onto neutral structure. But this fails to account for the persistence and universality of form across domains and observers.

The same geometric relations recur regardless of who observes them. The same harmonic structures arise whether or not they are interpreted. Order precedes recognition.

Intelligibility, therefore, cannot originate solely in the observer.[13] It must belong to reality itself.

Metaphysical light names this belonging.

Light and Vibration

The introduction of metaphysical light does not replace vibration as the operative process. It grounds it.

Vibration explains how form differentiates.

Light explains why that differentiation is intelligible.

Metaphysical light is not another vibration among vibrations. It is the ontological condition that allows vibration to articulate meaningfully rather than chaotically.[14]

Without it, vibration would yield motion but not form; repetition but not coherence; activity but not order.

Against Reduction

At this point, two reductions must be resisted:

1. Reducing metaphysical light to physical light

2. Reducing intelligibility to mental construction

The first confuses levels of explanation.

The second confuses recognition with origin.

Metaphysical light is not physical energy, yet it can become physically effective by articulating itself through vibration, geometry, and perceptual structures. Its effects are empirical, even if its source is not instrumentally detectable.[15]

This is not an appeal to mystery. It is an ontological clarification.

What This Chapter Establishes

This chapter has introduced, with necessity rather than assertion, the principle required to account for what has already been shown:

- Physical light enables visibility.

- Metaphysical light enables intelligibility.

- Form requires both to appear as meaningful order.

- Vibration differentiates; light discloses.

With this distinction in place, the demonstrations of earlier chapters are no longer isolated phenomena. They are unified under a single ontological condition.

Transition

If metaphysical light grounds intelligibility, then meaning cannot be extrinsic to form.

The next chapter turns to semiotics—not as convention, but as participation in intelligible structure.

Chapter 5
Vibration as Ontological Process

The preceding chapters have shown that form appears wherever vibration stabilizes, and that intelligibility requires more than physical illumination alone. What remains is to clarify the status of vibration itself.

Vibration must now be understood not merely as a physical event, but as an ontological process—the means by which intelligibility becomes articulated as form.[16]

If metaphysical light is the condition of intelligibility, vibration is the mode of its expression.

Vibration Beyond Motion

In common usage, vibration is often reduced to oscillatory motion in a physical medium. While this description is accurate within its domain, it is insufficient to account for the role vibration plays across levels of reality.

Vibration is better understood as rhythmic differentiation: a process by which unity unfolds into relation without losing coherence.[17] Wherever differentiation occurs without fragmentation, vibration is at work.

This is why vibration appears across domains that share no material substrate:

- acoustic oscillation
- electromagnetic radiation
- neural rhythms
- geometric proportion
- conceptual articulation

What unites these is not matter, but patterned activity.

Figure 5.1

Oscillation as Differentiation

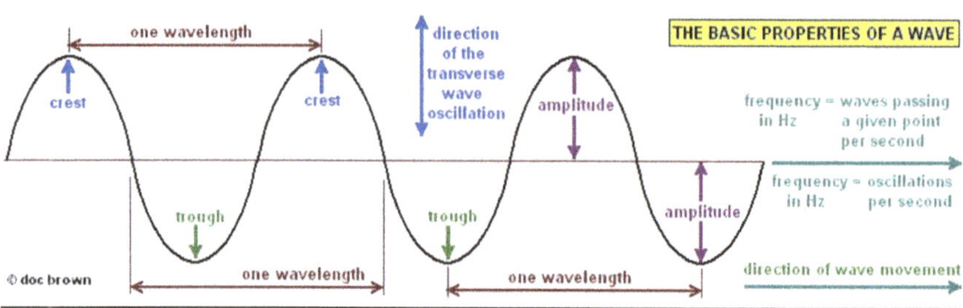

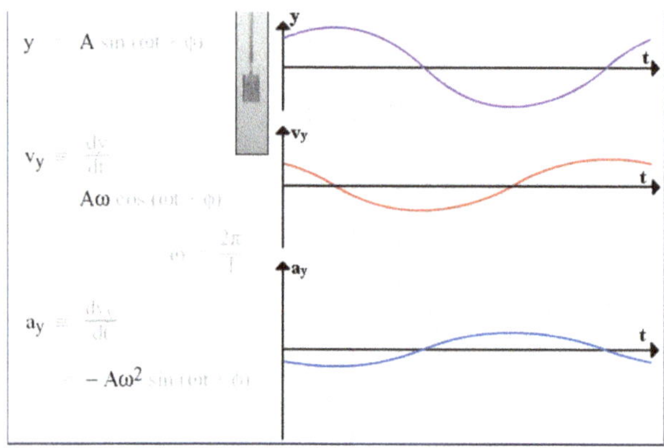

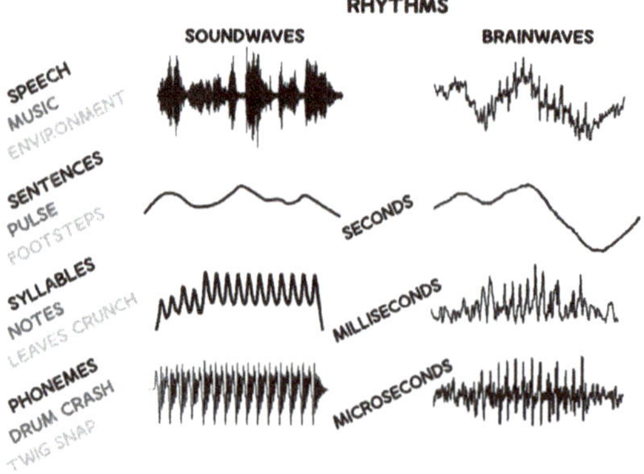

Oscillatory processes illustrating differentiation without disintegration.

Vibration differentiates without destroying unity. It introduces contrast—crest and trough, node and antinode—while preserving continuity. This capacity to differentiate without collapse is precisely what makes form possible.

Process Rather Than Substance

Form is often treated as a thing. Vibration reveals it to be an event.

A form persists only insofar as the process that sustains it continues. When the process ceases, the form dissolves. This is evident in cymatic figures, standing waves, and resonant structures: form is the visible trace of ongoing activity.

Ontology, therefore, cannot be grounded in static substance alone.[18] It must account for process as primary.

Vibration is that process.

Figure 5.2

Standing Waves as Sustained Form

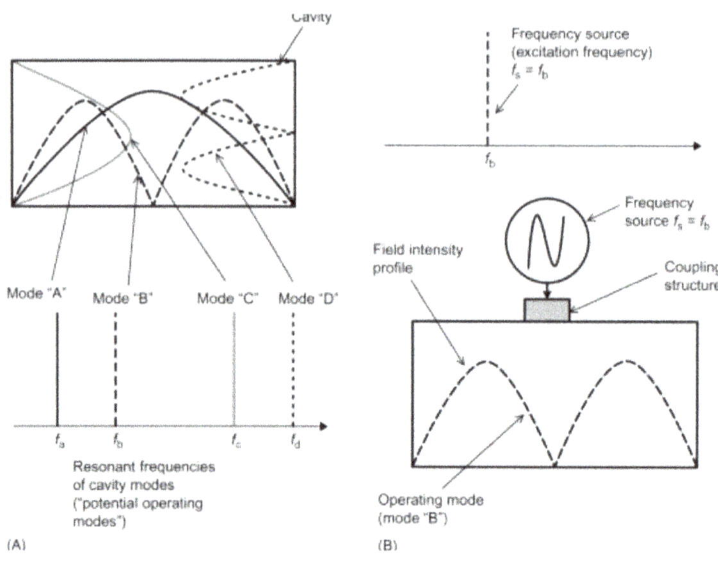

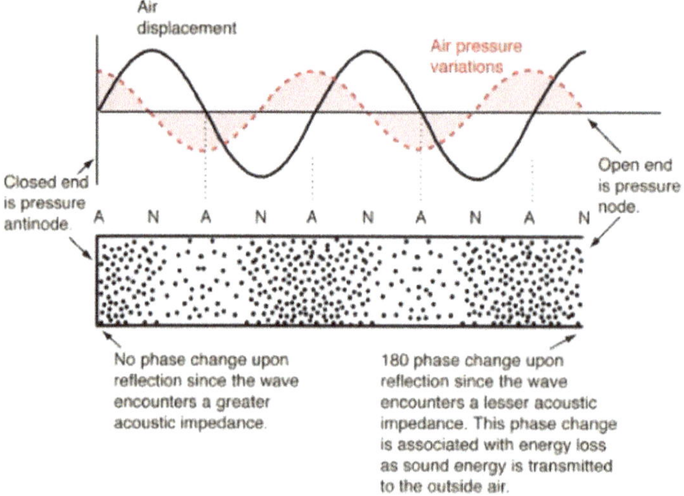

Standing waves showing form maintained through continuous oscillation.

Standing waves demonstrate how form can persist without material fixation. The pattern remains stable, yet nothing in it is still. Stability arises not from rest, but from balanced activity.

This balance is not accidental. It reflects a deeper ordering principle.

Vibration and Intelligible Order

Vibration alone does not guarantee form. Random oscillation yields noise. Form emerges only when vibration is ordered—when it conforms to relations that can sustain coherence.

This is where metaphysical light enters decisively.

Metaphysical light does not initiate vibration as an external cause. Rather, it orients vibration toward intelligibility.[19] It is the condition under which differentiation becomes articulation rather than dispersion.

In this sense:

- Vibration is the how of form

- Metaphysical light is the why of intelligibility

Neither is reducible to the other.

Figure 5.3

Coherence Versus Noise

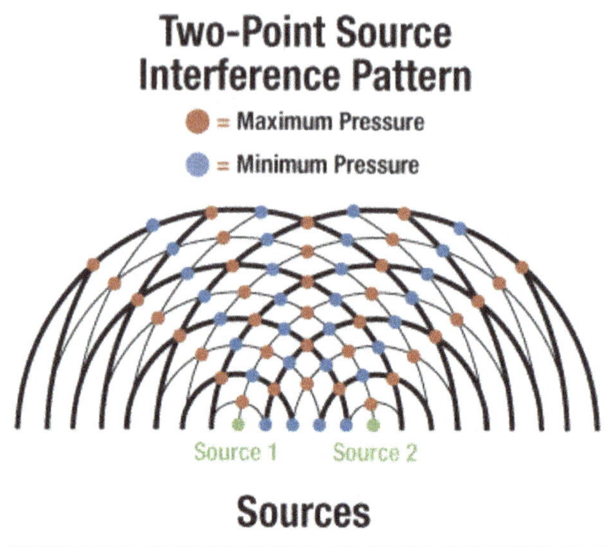

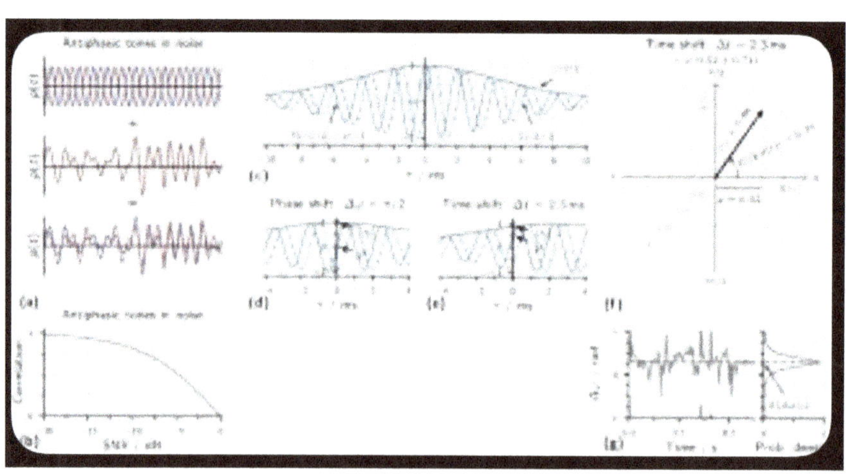

Comparison between coherent oscillation and random noise.

Where coherence is present, form appears. Where coherence is absent, vibration collapses into noise. The distinction is not imposed from outside; it arises from the internal relations of the system itself.

Coherence is therefore not accidental. It is ontologically significant.[20]

Self-Articulation Rather Than Imposition

Vibration does not receive form from without. It articulates form from within.

This articulation is self-determining. The system responds to its own constraints and possibilities. Metaphysical light is not an external designer, but the immanent condition that allows articulation to occur intelligibly.[21]

Thus form is neither arbitrary nor imposed. It is self-manifesting order.

What This Chapter Establishes

This chapter has clarified what must be true if the preceding demonstrations are to be coherent:

- Vibration is an ontological process, not merely physical motion.

- Form is sustained activity, not static substance.

- Vibration is an ontological process, not merely physical motion.

- Form is sustained activity, not static substance.

- Coherence distinguishes form from noise.

- Metaphysical light grounds intelligibility without replacing process.

Together, metaphysical light and vibration constitute a unified account of how form can appear as meaningful order.

Transition

If vibration is the process of articulation, and metaphysical light is the condition of intelligibility, then meaning cannot be externally assigned to form.

Meaning must be intrinsic.

The next chapter turns explicitly to semiotics—not as convention, but as participation in intelligible structure.

Part III - Why meaning is intrinsic

Chapter 6
Signs That Mean by Being

If form arises through vibration, and if vibration is oriented toward intelligibility by metaphysical light, then meaning cannot be an external addition to form. It cannot be assigned after the fact, nor imposed by agreement alone. Meaning must belong to form by virtue of what form is.

This claim is not metaphorical. It names an ontological condition. Beings are articulated; relations are grammatical in a deep sense; form possesses syntax—proportion, rhythm, differentiation—and meaning is intrinsic rather than assigned.

This is why geometry "speaks," color "communicates," and form "means." Not because these phenomena mimic human speech, but because human speech is a late crystallization of an already articulated reality.

For Plato, Logos is the primordial Language of intelligible articulation; human speech is derivative and can either participate in that articulation or drift into convention detached from reality.[22]

This is Logos as primordial Language.

This chapter makes that claim explicit.

A sign is not first an empty shape that later acquires significance.[23] A sign is a formed articulation of intelligibility. It means not because it points elsewhere, but because it participates in order.

Against the Arbitrariness of Signs

Modern semiotics often begins from the assumption that the relation between sign and meaning is arbitrary. On this view, forms are neutral carriers, and meaning is conferred by convention, usage, or mental association.

Ferdinand de Saussure's view that the bond between signifier (form/sound) and signified (concept) is arbitrary, based on social convention rather than inherent properties. Quote: "The connection between the signifier and the signified is arbitrary." While Saussure's structural linguistics posits signs as differential and arbitrary, this overlooks how vibration discloses form as inherently meaningful, as seen in cymatic patterns where geometry emerges without convention."

Such an account may describe certain linguistic practices, but it cannot explain why forms are intelligible at all. It presupposes meaning rather than accounting for its origin.

If meaning were purely arbitrary, no form would be intrinsically readable. Yet form is readable everywhere: in geometry, in rhythm, in proportion, in pattern, and in perceptual organization. Recognition precedes convention.[24] Contemporary materialist accounts often argue that intelligibility emerges solely from sufficient complexity—for example, through neural computation, evolutionary utility, or large-scale information processing. On such views, meaning and qualitative structure are late-stage byproducts rather than intrinsic features of form. This book does not deny emergence in this descriptive sense; it denies that emergence alone accounts for intelligibility as such. Complexity can explain functional organization, but it does not explain why organized structures are readable, coherent, or meaningful rather than merely operative. The present argument therefore concerns not causal sufficiency, but ontological grounding.

Figure 6.1

Non-Arbitrary Form Recognition

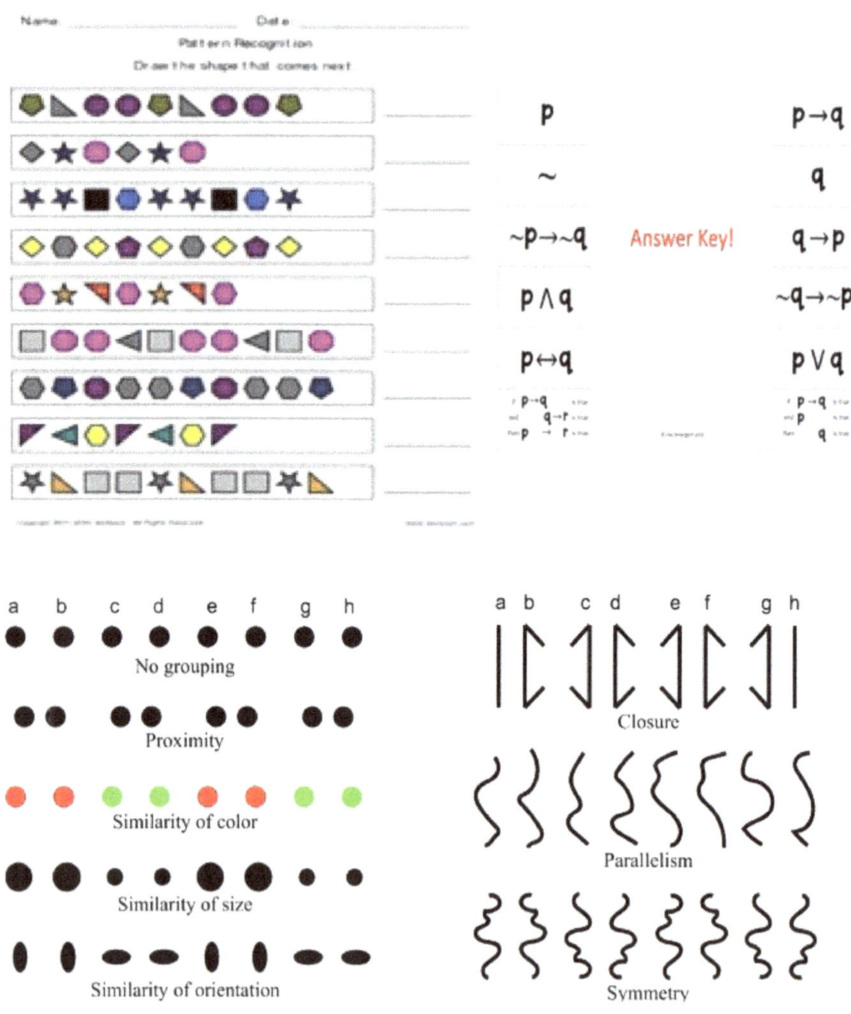

Forms that are immediately intelligible without prior convention.

Certain forms communicate structure directly. Balance, symmetry, repetition, and proportion are grasped without translation. They do not require decoding; they disclose themselves.

This disclosure is not subjective projection. It is the recognition of intrinsic order.

Form and Meaning Are Not Separate

Meaning is often treated as something layered on top of form: a mental interpretation applied to a neutral shape. But the demonstrations of earlier chapters show that form itself is already articulated, already differentiated, already ordered. Form is not imposed upon vibration; it is what vibration becomes when coherent. Signs, therefore, mean by being— their intelligibility arises from this intrinsic disclosure, not from arbitrary convention. [25] This holds across domains, from acoustic patterns to semiotic structures.

Where order is present, meaning is present.[26]

Form is meaningful because it is an expression of intelligible differentiation. Its structure is not mute. It speaks by being what it is.[27]

Figure 6.2

Proportion as Meaningful Relation

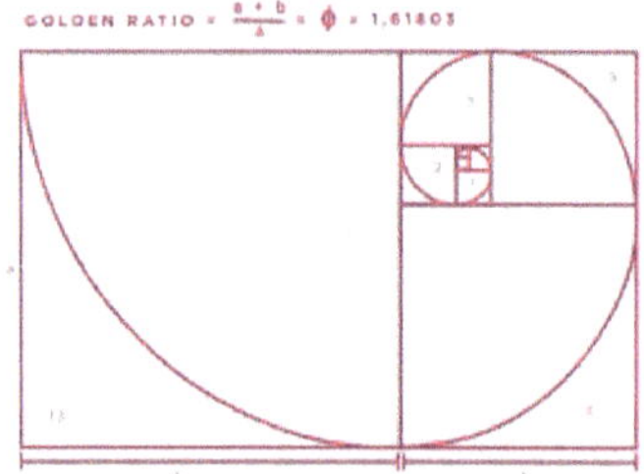

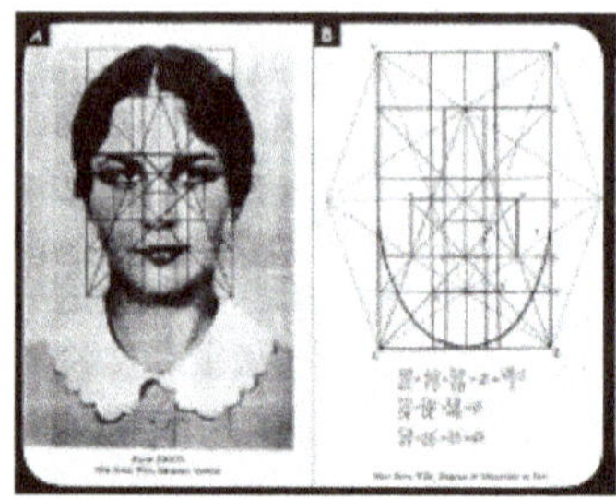

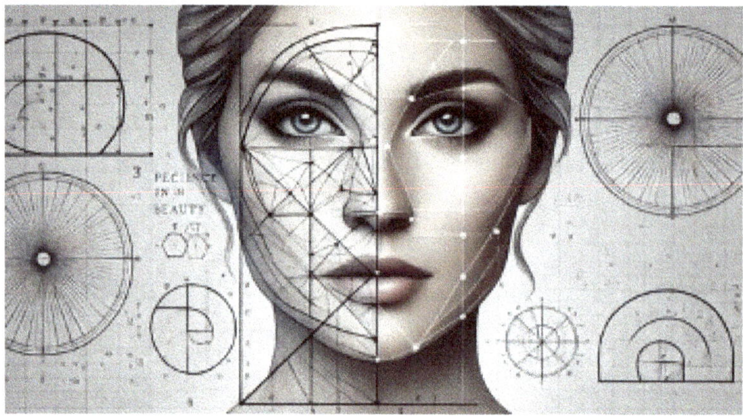

Proportional relations perceived as meaningful without symbolic mediation.

Proportion is not merely numerical. It is relational coherence. A proportion holds because it resolves tensions within a whole. That resolution is perceived as fitting, balanced, or complete.

Meaning here is not symbolic reference. It is structural rightness.

Light as the Medium of Signification

Meaning does not arise in darkness. It requires disclosure.

Physical light enables visibility, but metaphysical light enables signification.[28] It is the medium in which form can appear as intelligible rather than opaque.

Signs therefore emerge where form is disclosed through light. This disclosure is not metaphorical. It is ontological. Metaphysical light makes articulation possible; physical light allows it to be perceived.

A sign is thus a meeting point:

- of vibration (process),
- of form (structure),
- and of light (intelligibility).

Intrinsic Meaning

Why Convention Cannot Be Primary.

Conventions presuppose shared recognition. Shared recognition presupposes intelligible form. Therefore, convention cannot be the origin of meaning.[29]

This does not deny that conventions exist. It denies that they are foundational.

Conventions refine, constrain, and specialize meaning. They do not create it.

Figure 6.3

Intrinsic Meaning Across Domains

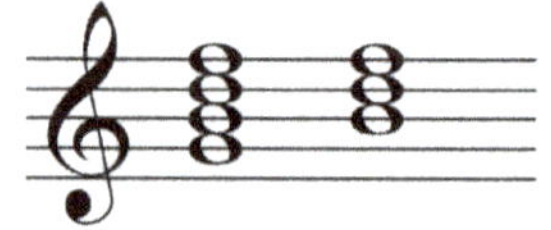

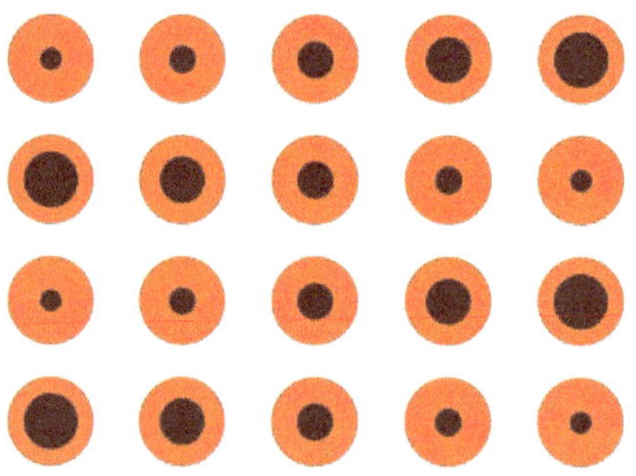

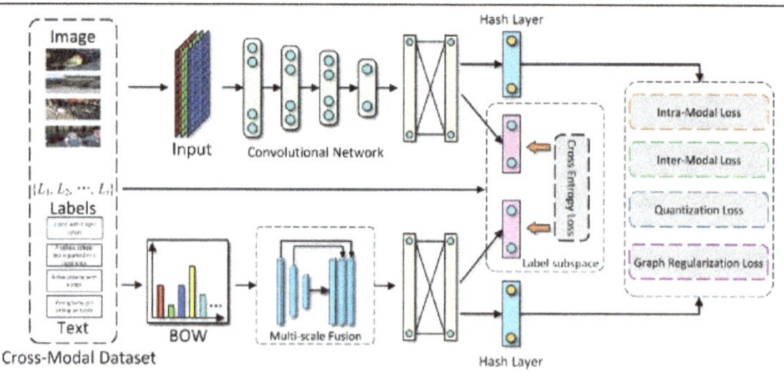

Chapter 7
Where Is Color?

Few questions reveal the limits of modern theories of perception as clearly as a simple one: where is color?

Is red located in the object, in the light, or in the mind? Each answer seems plausible, yet each proves insufficient when taken alone. Objects do not contain color independently of illumination. Light does not carry color as a property, only as wavelength. The mind does not invent color arbitrarily, for color perception is lawful, repeatable, and constrained.

Color appears, yet it resists localization.[30]

This resistance is not a failure of explanation. It is a clue.

Figure 7.2

Color as Interaction Rather Than Location

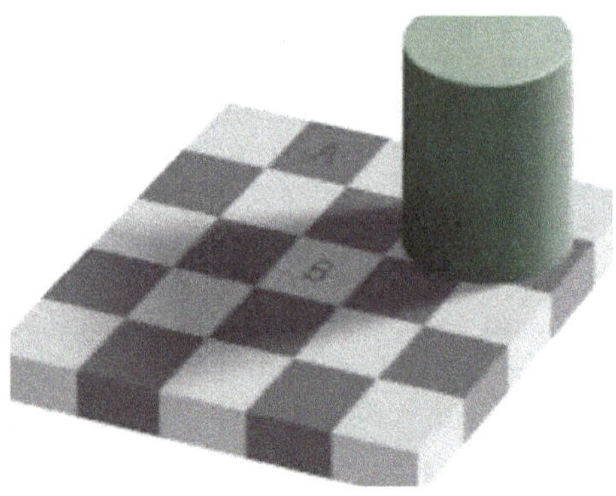

Color Illumination

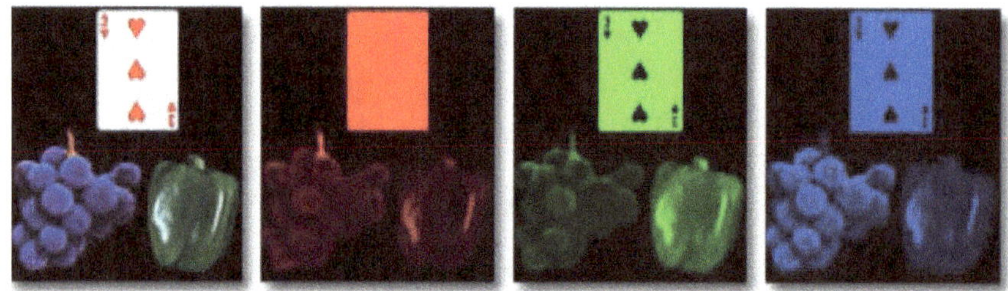

Figure 2

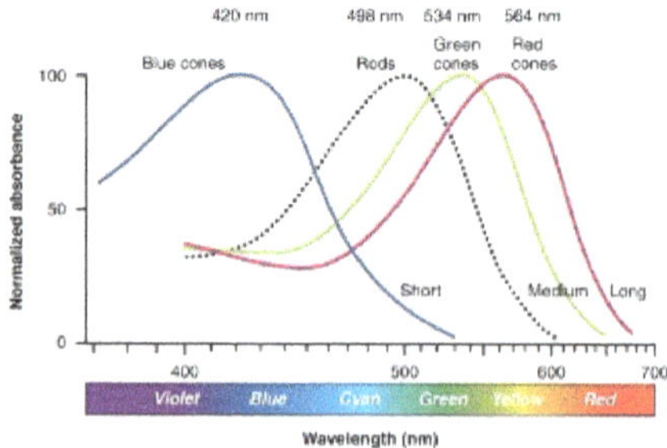

Color appearing differently under varying illumination, despite unchanged physical objects.

When illumination changes, color changes. The object remains the same, yet its appearance shifts. This alone shows that color is not a fixed property of matter.

At the same time, color perception is not arbitrary. Under comparable conditions, observers reliably report similar colors. This regularity shows that color is not a subjective invention.

Color therefore belongs neither solely to object nor solely to mind. It belongs to the relation.[31]

Physical Light and Perceptual Coding

From the standpoint of physics, light consists of electromagnetic waves of varying wavelengths. From the standpoint of physiology, these wavelengths stimulate photoreceptors in the retina, initiating neural activity. From the standpoint of neuroscience, this activity is encoded as patterns—sometimes described as a "brain code."

Each description is accurate within its domain. None, however, accounts for the experience of color itself.

Wavelength is not redness. Neural firing is not blueness.[32] The descriptions explain conditions, not appearance.

Figure 7.2

Neural Encoding and Color Experience

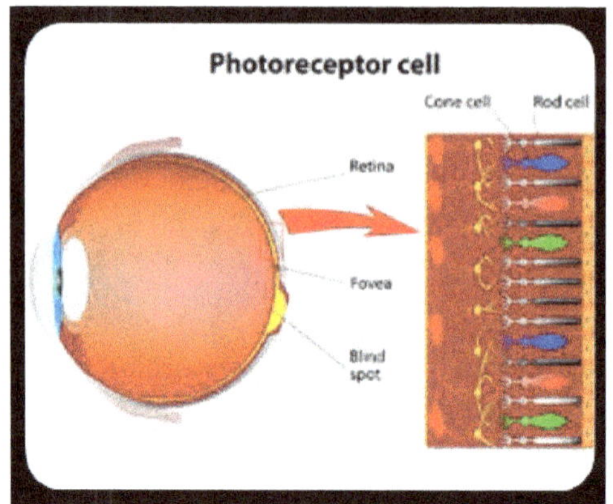

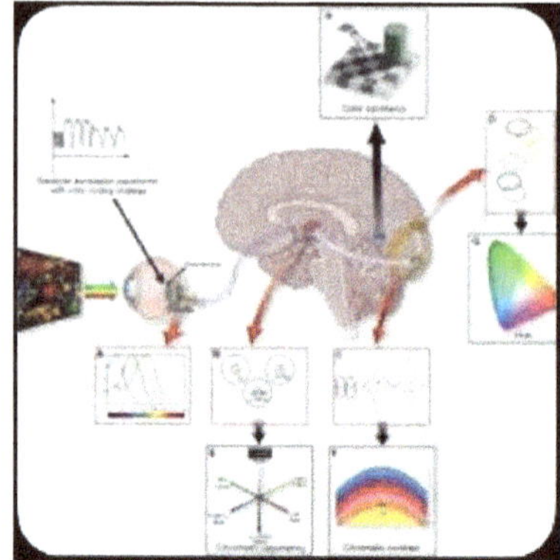

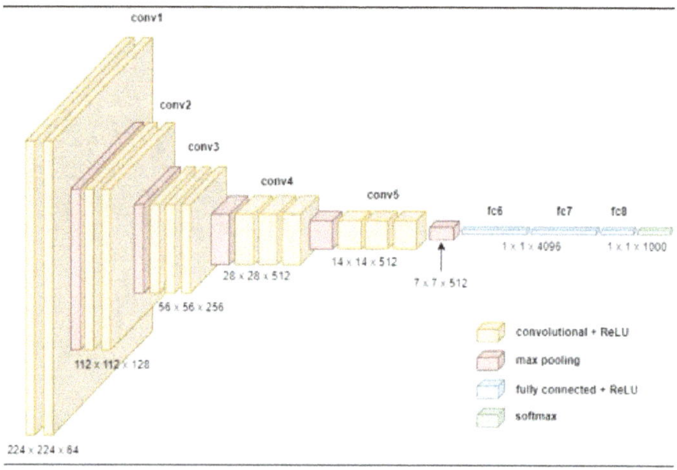

Physiological processes enabling color perception without containing color as such.

Color does not reside in the retina or the cortex as a thing. It appears through these processes, not within them.

The same structure encountered earlier reappears here: vibration differentiated through light becomes intelligible form.

Color as Disclosed Form

Perception Beyond Localization

Color is not a secondary illusion layered on top of a neutral world. It is a mode of disclosure.[33]

Through color, form announces itself. Boundaries become perceptible. Depth appears. Relations are revealed. Color articulates space.

This articulation is intelligible. It is not chaotic sensation. Color carries meaning—warmth and coolness, advance and recession, emphasis and harmony—without requiring translation.

Color therefore functions as a sign, but one whose meaning is intrinsic.[34]

Figure 7.3

Color as Structural Differentiation

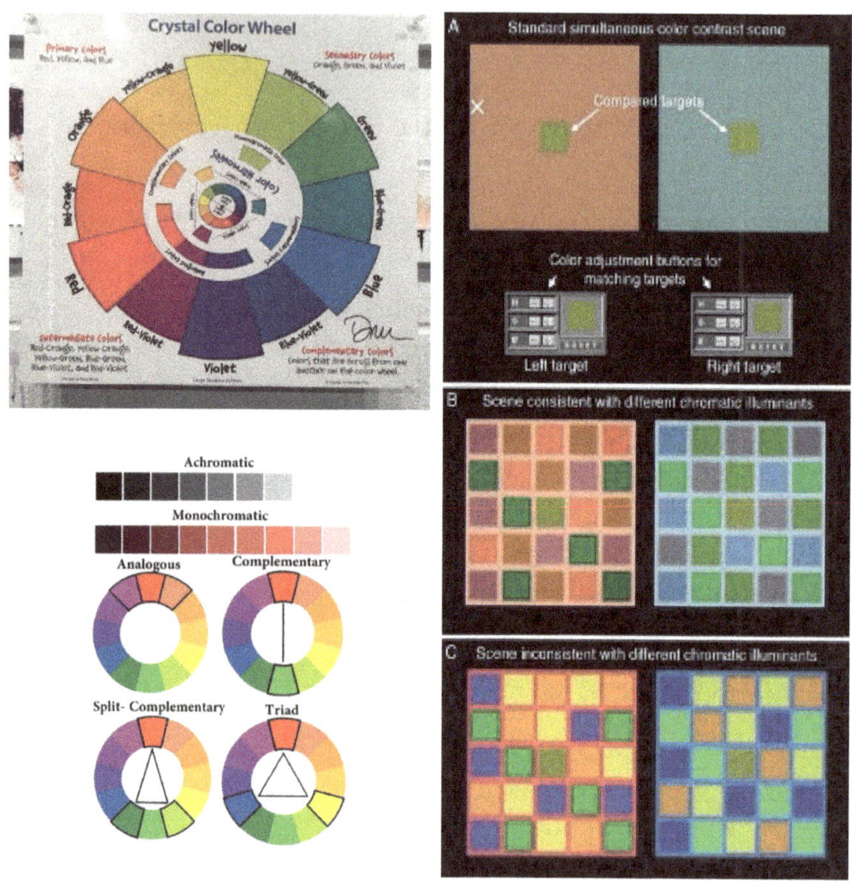

Color organizing visual form through contrast, harmony, and proportion.

Artists have always understood this. Color is not applied to form; it is form in its luminous aspect. To see color well is to see structure.

This is why aesthetic perception cannot be reduced to passive reception. To perceive color is to participate in the articulation of intelligible order.

Perception as Participation

If color cannot be located in object, light, or mind alone, then perception must be understood differently.

Color is neither a subjective illusion nor a mere property of objects; it is disclosed in the coherence of light's interaction with form. Qualia emerge not as private ineffable but as relational participations in this luminosity. [35] Afterimages, for instance, reveal color's persistence beyond immediate stimulus, underscoring its ontological status.

Perception is not the mind constructing a world from neutral inputs. Nor is it the world imprinting itself mechanically upon the senses. Perception is participation in a process.[36]

Metaphysical light grounds intelligibility. Physical light enables visibility. Neural processes mediate articulation. Color appears where these converge.

Perception, therefore, is neither subjective projection nor objective imprint. It is co-presence.

The Aesthetic Consequence

If perception is participation, then aesthetics is not concerned merely with preference or taste. It concerns the degree to which intelligible form becomes perceptible.

The aesthetic experience of color is a moment in which metaphysical light becomes sensibly manifest through physical light and perceptual form.[37] The experience is real, structured, and meaningful.

This is why color can move, orient, and disclose—without argument.

What This Chapter Establishes

This chapter has shown that:

- Color cannot be localized as a property of object or mind alone.

- Color arises through the interaction of light, form, and perception.

- Perception is participatory rather than representational.

- Aesthetic experience is a mode of access to intelligible structure.

Color is therefore not an illusion. It is a luminous articulation of form.

Transition

If perception is participation in intelligible structure, then those most attuned to form are not merely observers—they are witnesses.

The next chapter turns to the figure who embodies this attunement: the artist.

Part IV - Perception As Participation

Chapter 8

The Enlightened Artist

If perception is participation in intelligible structure, then not all perceivers participate to the same degree. Attunement varies. Sensitivity varies. What differs is not access to reality, but clarity of reception.

This chapter addresses the figure who exemplifies such clarity: the artist—not as a producer of subjective expression, but as a witness to form.

The term enlightened is used here with philosophical precision. It does not denote moral superiority, mystical privilege, or personal revelation. It names a condition of perception in which intelligible structure becomes consistently perceptible.[38]

Plato and the Misreading of Art

Plato is often cited as an enemy of art.[39] This reading depends on a confusion between imitation and disclosure.

Plato's criticism is directed not at form, but at copies severed from intelligibility. When art merely reproduces appearances without understanding their ordering principle, it multiplies illusion. When art participates in intelligibility, it does the opposite.[40]

The artist Plato distrusts is not the one who sees too deeply, but the one who does not see deeply enough.

Figure 8.1

Artistic Form as Disclosure

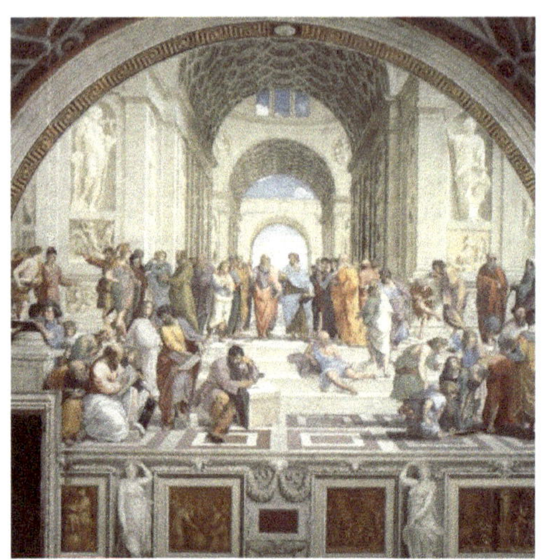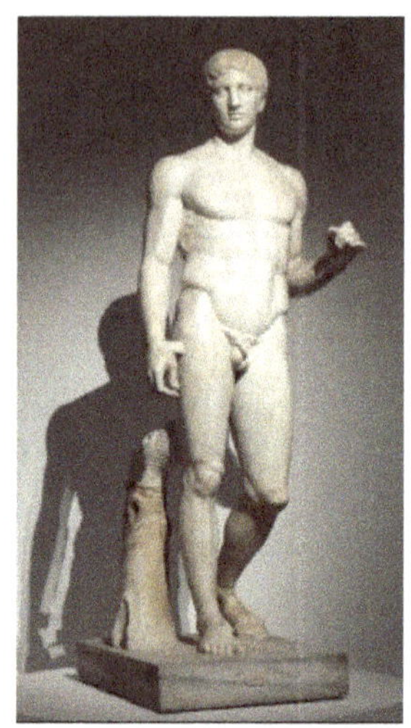

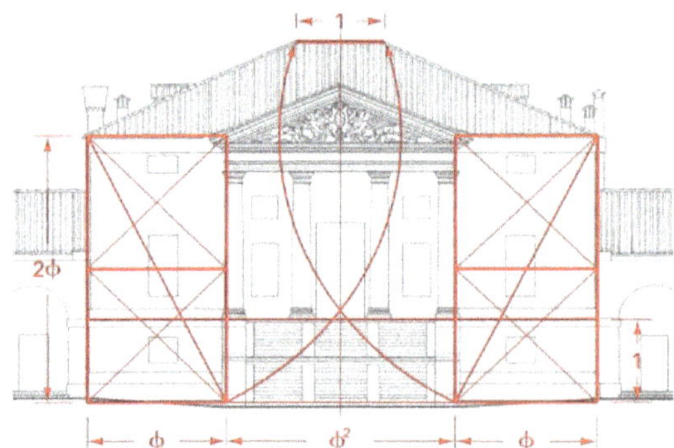

Artworks in which proportion and form disclose intelligible order rather than sur-face likeness.

Where art is governed by proportion, rhythm, balance, and luminosity, it does not imitate reality—it reveals it. Such works are not expressive in the psychological sense. They are structural.

This distinction is decisive.

The Artist as Perceptual Instrument

The artist is often described as a creator. More accurately, the artist is a receiver—a refined perceptual instrument attuned to form. [41]

The artist does not impose meaning but participates in the disclosure of form through disciplined attention.

Just as a sensitive membrane responds more precisely to vibration, a trained perception responds more clearly to intelligible structure. What distinguishes the artist is not imagination alone, but fidelity to what appears.

The artist does not impose meaning. Meaning arrives.

Everyday Attunement and Empirical Insights

Cognitive studies illustrate this: Repeated practice refines perceptual attunement, as in musicians discerning microtonal pitches or artists perceiving nuanced color gradients—mirroring how vibration discloses form.[42] Consider digital fractals: Algorithmic vibration generates infinite forms, disclosed not passively but through active exploration, much like an artist's canvas interaction. [43] In vernier tasks, training yields hyperacuity, where perception exceeds physical hardware—analogous to light's coherence revealing forms beyond mere sensation. [44]

Figure 8.2

Rhythm, Proportion, and Attunement

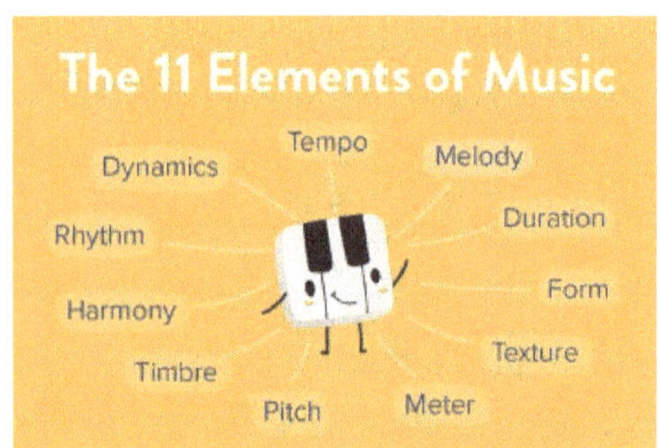

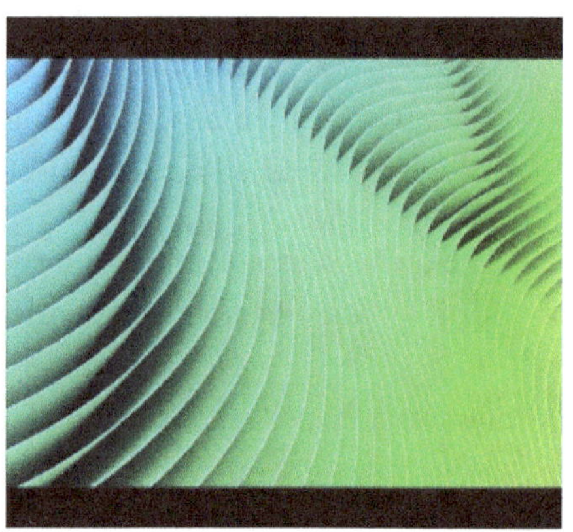

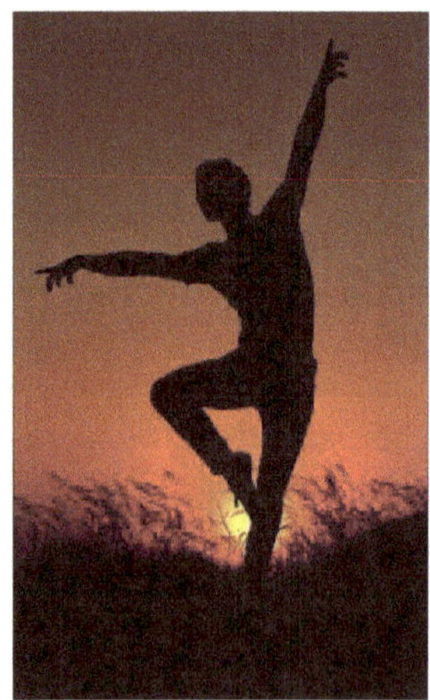

Rhythmic structures across artistic media revealing coherence rather than expression.

Rhythm in music, balance in composition, cadence in language— these are not decorative choices. They are recognitions of order. The artist perceives relations before naming them.

This is why art often precedes theory.[45] Form is seen before it is explained.

Enlightenment as Perceptual Clarity

To be enlightened, in this context, is to perceive form without obstruction.

Metaphysical light is not absent from ordinary perception. It is simply obscured by habit, distraction, and conceptual overlay. The enlightened artist is one who has removed those obstructions—not by withdrawing from the world, but by attending more carefully to it.

Enlightenment here is not transcendence of perception, but its refinement.[46]

Art as Ontological Testimony

Artworks endure not because they entertain, but because they testify. They show what intelligible order looks like when it becomes perceptible. This is why certain works remain compelling across centuries and cultures. Their meaning is not conventional. It is structural.[47]

They continue to speak because they participate in the same intelligible light that grounds perception itself.

Light in art does more than reveal surfaces. It shapes volume, discloses depth, and orders space. Artists who understand light do not paint illumination; they compose intelligibility.

This use of light mirrors the ontological distinction established earlier: physical light reveals, metaphysical light discloses.

Figure 8.3

Light as Form in Art

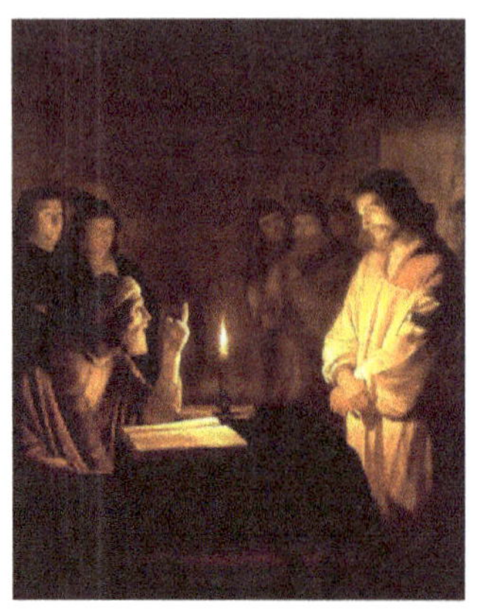

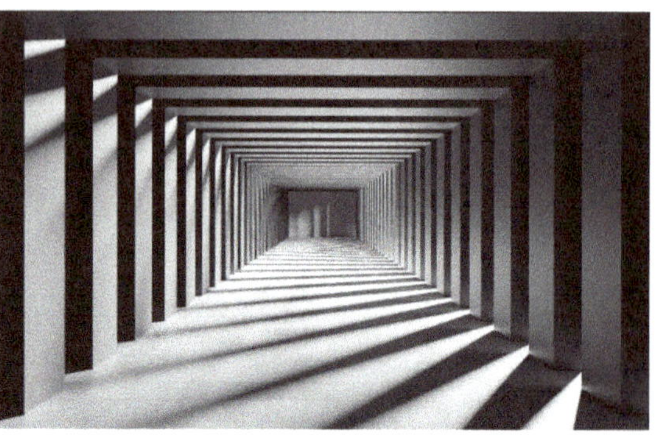

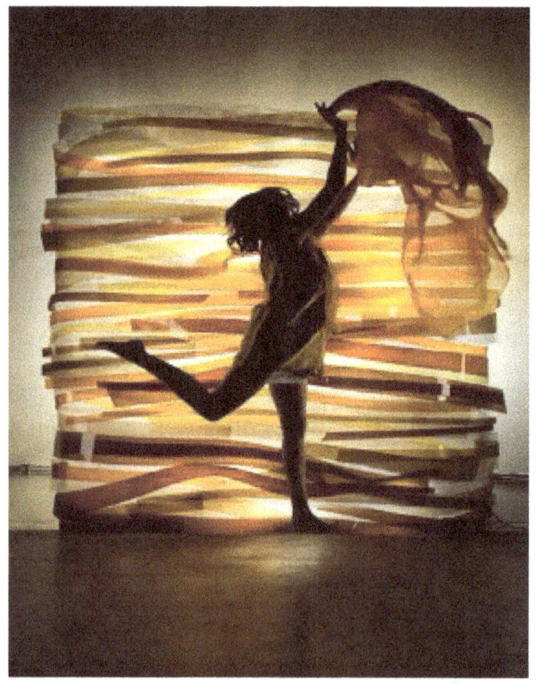

Light used in art not merely to illuminate, but to articulate form.

This distinction is increasingly visible in contemporary digital and algorithmic practices, where form may be generated automatically yet remains intelligible only when coherence, proportion, and disclosure are preserved. Even where authorship is distributed or obscured, intelligibility is not produced by computation alone, but by the articulation of form within constraints that sustain meaning.

Against Subjective Expression

Modern aesthetics often frames art as expression of inner states. While expression may occur, it cannot be primary.

If art were primarily expressive, its meaning would be private and transient. Yet great art is public and enduring. It communicates because it articulates order that others can recognize.

Expression follows recognition. It does not replace it.[48]

What This Chapter Establishes

This chapter has shown that:

- The artist is a witness to intelligible structure.

- Artistic perception is participatory, not projective.

- Enlightenment refers to perceptual clarity, not mysticism.

- Art discloses ontology rather than expressing psychology.

The artist stands not outside reality, but closer to its articulation.

Transition

If art testifies to intelligible order, then the fragmentation of modern disciplines appears increasingly artificial.

The final chapters ask what follows if this account of form, meaning, and perception is taken seriously.

Chapter 9

Against Fragmentation

Modern knowledge is divided. Physics, biology, neuroscience, linguistics, aesthetics, and philosophy proceed as though they occupy separate territories, governed by distinct principles and methods. Each discipline develops its own vocabulary, its own standards of explanation, and its own criteria of validity.

This division is often taken to reflect the structure of reality itself.

The preceding chapters suggest otherwise.

What has been shown repeatedly is that the same ordering process operates across domains. Vibration articulates form; light discloses intelligibility; geometry stabilizes relation; meaning emerges intrinsically; perception participates. These are not isolated findings. They are manifestations of a single ontological continuity.

Fragmentation, therefore, does not originate in reality. It originates in method.[49]

The Historical Source of Division

The division of knowledge into discrete disciplines is a relatively recent development.[50] In classical natural philosophy, inquiries into nature, form, meaning, and perception were not separate enterprises. They were aspects of a single attempt to understand how order appears.

The modern separation of domains arose alongside the success of instrumental explanation. Measurement, quantification, and specialization yielded extraordinary predictive power. But they also encouraged a narrowing of explanatory scope.[51]

What could not be easily measured was bracketed.

What could not be localized was deferred.

What could not be isolated was excluded.

Intelligibility itself became an afterthought.

Figure 9.1

Fragmented Versus Unified Knowledge

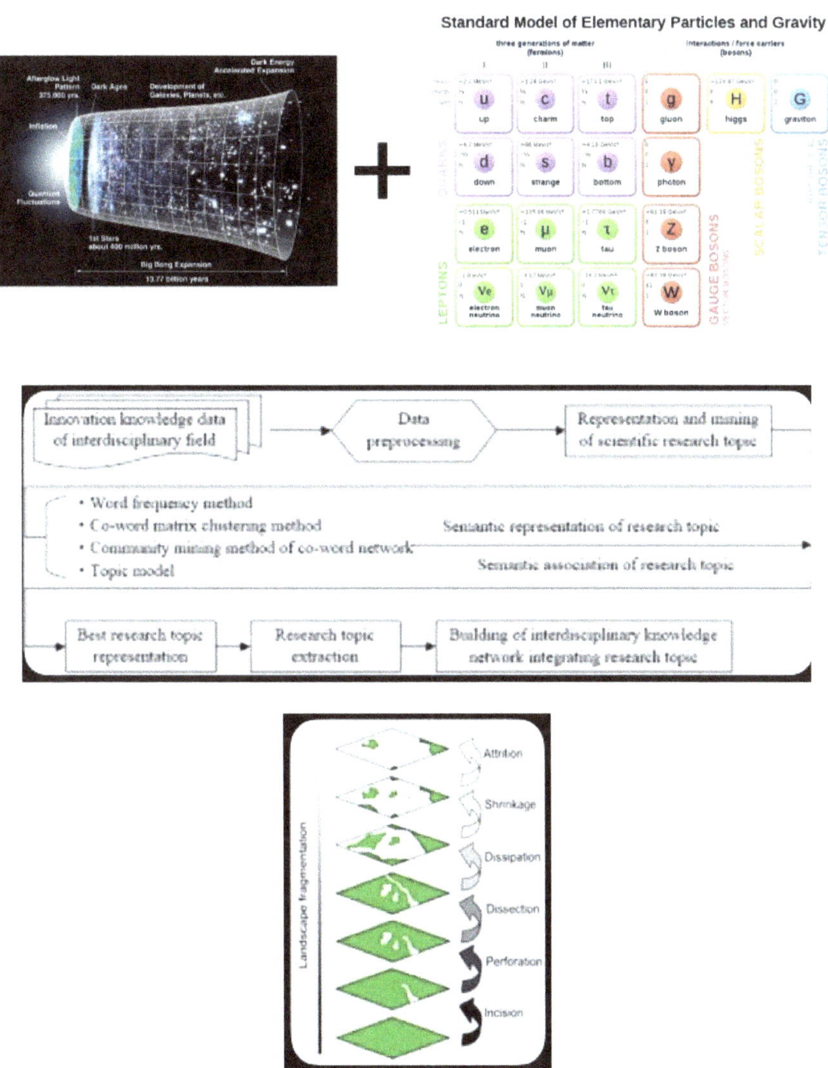

Contrasting models of knowledge: isolated domains versus integrated structure.

In the fragmented model, each discipline explains its objects internally while presupposing what it does not explain. Physics presupposes intelligibility. Neuroscience presupposes meaning. Semiotics presupposes perception. Aesthetics presupposes form.

Each depends on what another excludes.

Why Reduction Fails

Fragmentation is often defended through reduction: the claim that higher-level phenomena can be fully explained in terms of lower level processes. Meaning becomes reducible to neural activity; perception to computation; form to material interaction.

But reduction explains conditions without accounting for appearance as such.[52]

Neural firing does not explain why form is intelligible.

Electromagnetic waves do not explain why geometry recurs.

Computation does not explain why structure is meaningful.

Reduction displaces the problem rather than resolving it.

Unity Without Collapse

To reject fragmentation is not to collapse disciplines into one another. Physics does not become aesthetics. Neuroscience does not become metaphysics. Each retains its proper domain and method.

What changes is the ontological horizon.

Disciplines are re-situated as partial articulations of a unified process, not as isolated explanations. Their findings become complementary rather than competitive.

Unity here is not uniformity. It is coherence.[53]

Figure 9.2

Levels of Articulation

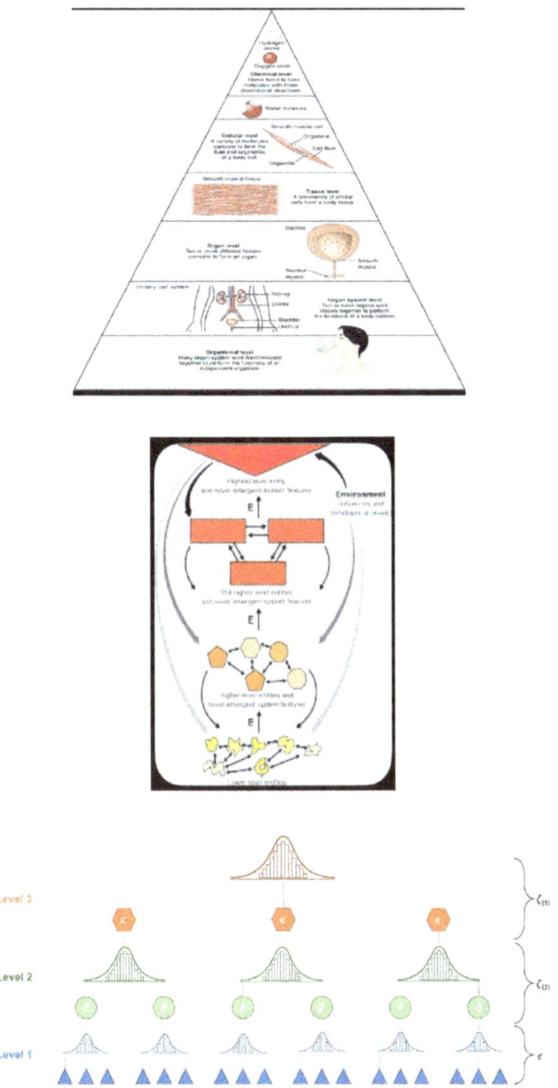

Distinct levels of articulation operating within a single ontological process.

Metaphysical light grounds intelligibility.

Vibration differentiates.

Form stabilizes.

Meaning emerges.

Perception participates.

Each level articulates the same reality under different conditions.

The Cost of Fragmentation

Unity Without Reduction

When disciplines proceed in isolation, several consequences follow:

- Meaning is treated as subjective or secondary.

- Aesthetics is marginalized as non-cognitive.

- Ontology is reduced to material description.

- Perception is explained without appearance.

The result is not clarity, but impoverishment.

Reality becomes unintelligible precisely where it is most structured.

Recovering Unity Amid Fragmentation

In our fractured age, reality appears disjointed, but intrinsic coherence counters this—meaning is not subsystem-bound but universally disclosed through vibration-to-form. [54] This ontology restores harmony without denying diversity.

A Return to Natural Philosophy

What is required is not a new synthesis imposed from above, but a recovery of an older orientation: natural philosophy understood as the study of how intelligible order appears.[55]

This orientation does not reject science. It situates science within a broader ontological field. Measurement becomes one mode of access among others, not the sole arbiter of reality.

Aesthetics, in this context, regains epistemic dignity.[56] It is no longer a matter of taste, but a domain in which intelligible structure becomes perceptible.

What This Chapter Establishes

This chapter has shown that:

- Fragmentation is methodological, not ontological.
- Reduction explains conditions but not intelligibility.
- Unity does not require collapse of disciplines.
- A recovered natural philosophy can integrate without erasing difference.

The divisions of modern knowledge are not reflections of reality's structure. They are artifacts of explanatory strategy.

Transition

If fragmentation is not necessary, then an alternative orientation is possible.

The final chapter asks what follows—philosophically, aesthetically, and practically—if reality is understood once again as an intelligible, articulated whole.

Part V - A Recovered Natural Philosophy

Chapter 10

A Classical Ontology for a Fractured Age

This book began with phenomena rather than theory. It ends with ontology—not as speculation, but as necessity.[57]

Form appears from vibration.

Vibration stabilizes into geometry.

Geometry is intelligible.

Meaning is intrinsic.

Perception participates.

Art testifies.

If these claims hold, then reality cannot be adequately understood as a collection of disconnected mechanisms. Nor can intelligibility be treated as a secondary effect of matter or mind. What has been shown requires a different orientation: one in which being is articulated, luminous, and inherently meaningful.

This orientation is not new. It is classical.[58]

Ontology Recovered, Not Invented

Classical ontology did not begin by asking what exists as isolated objects. It asked how order appears at all. Being was understood not as inert substance, but as articulated presence—as that which shows itself through form, proportion, and light.[59]

The demonstrations presented in this book return us to that insight. They do not revive it nostalgically; they confirm it empirically. The same principles recognized in ancient natural philosophy reappear whenever vibration organizes matter, whenever geometry stabilizes relation, and whenever meaning is perceived without convention.

Ontology, in this sense, is not a theory imposed upon experience. It is what experience discloses when attended to without reduction.[60]

Being appears not as a mute fact, but as structured intelligibility.

Logos is the immanent condition through which the world is continuously articulated. There is no outside to Logos, no before it, and no space in which it could be absent. What appears does so from within Logos as intelligible differentiation.[61]

Light, in its metaphysical sense, names this condition—not as an object among objects, but as the field of disclosure in which articulation becomes possible.[62]

Figure 10.1

Articulated Being

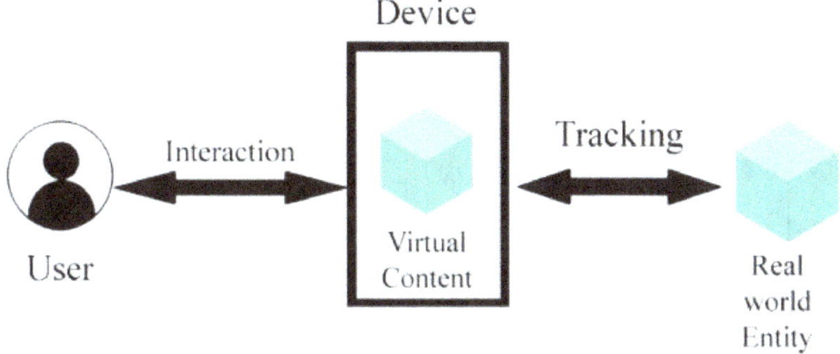

Augmented Reality Architecture

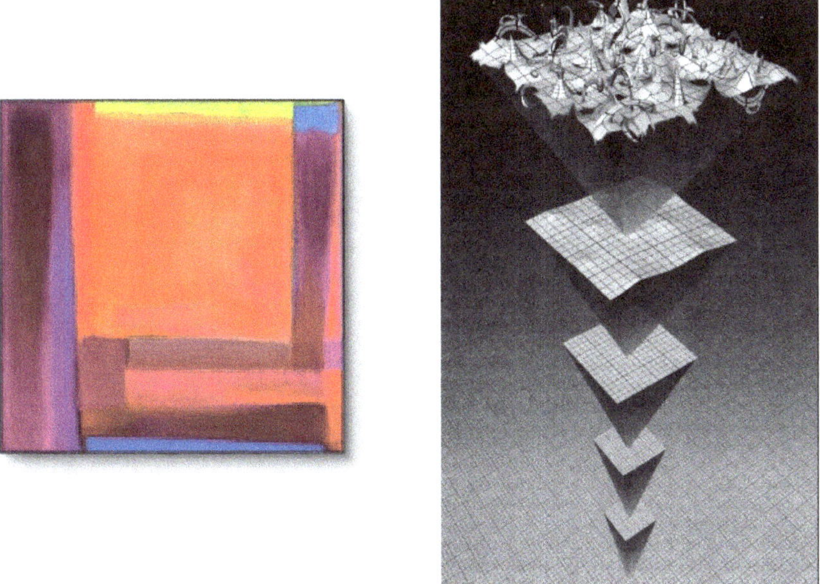

Being understood as articulated order rather than inert substance.

Light, Not as Metaphor, but as Principle

Throughout this book, light has been treated with care. It is not metaphorical ornament. Nor is it reducible to physical illumination alone.

Physical light enables visibility.

Metaphysical light enables intelligibility.

Without the former, appearance vanishes.

Without the latter, appearance becomes opaque.

Together, they account for how reality can be both present and meaningful.

This dual articulation does not introduce a dualism of worlds.[63] It introduces levels of articulation within a single reality. The physical and the intelligible are not opposed; they are coordinated.

Vibration as the Mode of Articulation

Vibration has emerged as the mode through which articulation occurs. Not as brute motion, but as rhythmic differentiation capable of coherence.

Vibration explains how unity becomes relation without fragmentation.[64] It accounts for why form is dynamic, why geometry recurs, and why meaning is not arbitrary. Vibration is the process through which metaphysical light becomes form.

Ontology, therefore, is not static. It is processual without being chaotic.

This coherence is not imposed from without. It is intrinsic to articulation itself. Where coherence persists, intelligibility persists. Where it collapses, form dissolves.

Figure 10.2

Coherent Differentiation

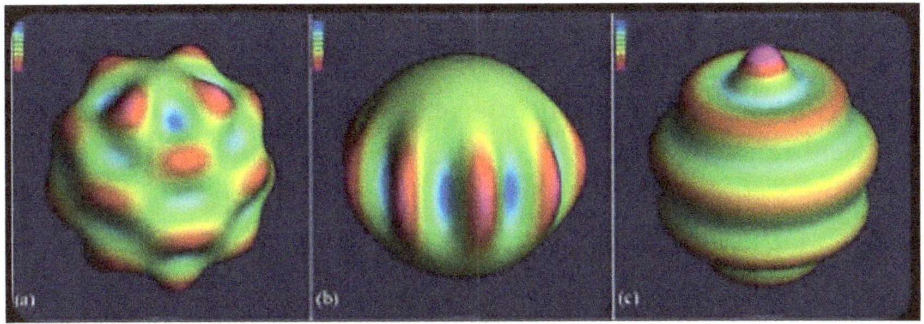

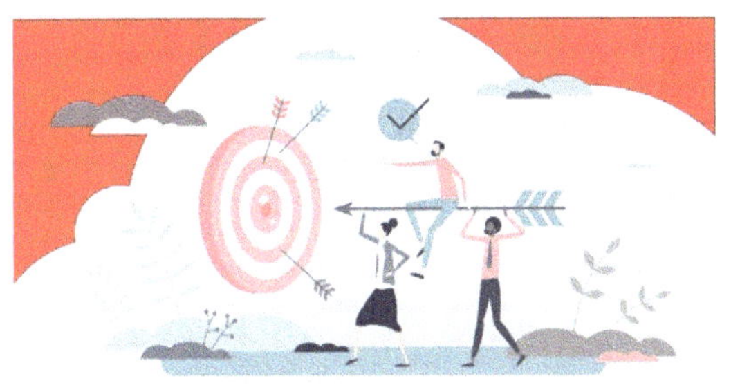

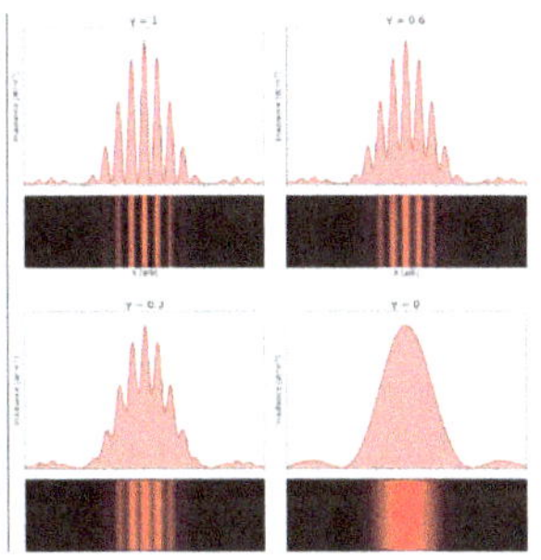

Differentiation that preserves coherence rather than dispersing into noise.

Meaning, Perception, and Art Reunified

If meaning is intrinsic to form, then perception is not a passive reception of data nor a projection of inner states. It is participation in intelligible order. Aesthetics, in turn, is not a marginal concern, but a domain in which this participation becomes especially clear.

Art occupies a privileged position here—not as subjective expression, but as ontological testimony.[65] Artworks endure because they disclose structure that others can recognize. They are not persuasive; they are evident.

This is why artists so often anticipate philosophical insight. They encounter order before it is named.

Against Final Explanations

This ontology does not promise final explanations. It resists closure.

Reality, understood as articulated intelligibility, cannot be exhausted by any single description. What it offers instead is orientation: a way of attending to phenomena that preserves their coherence without reducing them to fragments.[66]

Such an ontology does not compete with science. It grounds it. It does not replace specialized inquiry; it situates it. It does not dismiss modern achievements; it restores their context.

Figure 10.3

Integrated Orientation

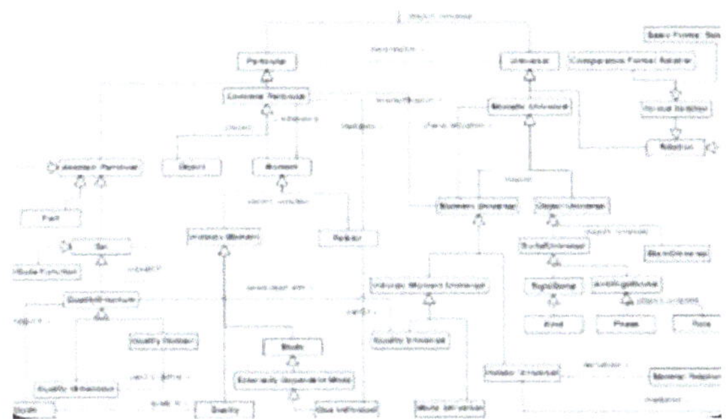

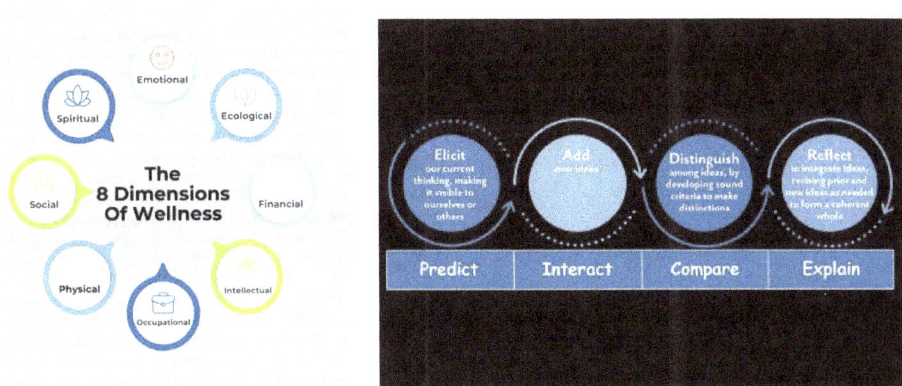

An orientation in which multiple domains articulate a single intelligible reality.

What Follows

If this account is sound, several consequences follow:

- Meaning is not subjective invention.

- Aesthetics is epistemically serious.

- Perception is participatory.

- Art is revelatory.

- Fragmentation is methodological, not ontological.

These are not new doctrines. They are recoveries.

Closing

This book has argued, by demonstration rather than decree, that reality is luminous before it is analyzed, articulated before it is explained, and meaningful before it is interpreted.

To recognize this is not to retreat from rigor. It is to restore it.

The task now is not to add another theory to an already crowded field, but to attend more carefully to what has always been present.

Form appears.

Meaning is intrinsic.

Light discloses.

Nothing further is required.

The End of Book

Notes

1. Plato, Timaeus, trans. Donald J. Zeyl (Indianapolis: Hackett Publishing Company, 2000).

2. Aristotle, Metaphysics, trans. W. D. Ross, in The Complete Works of Aristotle, vol. 2, ed. Jonathan Barnes (Princeton: Princeton University Press, 1984).

3. Plato, Republic, trans. G. M. A. Grube, rev. C. D. C. Reeve (Indianapolis: Hackett Publishing Company, 1992), bk. VI– VII.

4. Aristotle, Physics, trans. R. P. Hardie and R. K. Gaye, in The Complete Works of Aristotle, vol. 1, ed. Jonathan Barnes (Princeton: Princeton University Press, 1984).

5. Plato, Cratylus, trans. C. D. C. Reeve, in Plato: Complete Works, ed. John M. Cooper (Indianapolis: Hackett Publishing Company, 1997).

6. Plato, Republic, bk. VI.

7. Plato, Republic, bk. VII.

8. Aristotle, Metaphysics.

9. Plato, Timaeus.

10. Aristotle, Physics.

11. Plato, Republic, bk. VI–VII.

12. Aristotle, Metaphysics.

13. Plato, Cratylus.

14. Plato, Timaeus.

15. Aristotle, Metaphysics.

16. Plato, Republic, bk. VI–VII.

17. Aristotle, Physics.

18. Plato, Timaeus.

19. Plato, Republic, bk. VI.

20. Aristotle, Metaphysics.

21. Plato, Cratylus.

22. Aristotle, De Anima, trans. J. A. Smith, in The Complete Works of Aristotle, vol. 1, ed. Jonathan Barnes (Princeton: Princeton University Press, 1984).

23. Plato, Timaeus.

24. Aristotle, Metaphysics.

25. Ferdinand de Saussure, in Course in General Linguistics, edited by Charles Bally and Albert Sechehaye, translated by Wade Baskin (New York: Philosophical Library, 1959), posits the bond between signifier and signified as arbitrary and conventional (e.g., "The connection between the signifier and the signified is arbitrary"). This overlooks vibration's role in disclosing form as inherently meaningful, as cymatic patterns demonstrate geometry emerging without social imposition, resolving arbitrariness through ontological coherence.

26. Plato, Republic, bk. VII.

27. Aristotle, Physics.

28. Plato, Cratylus.

29. Plato, Timaeus.

30. Aristotle, Metaphysics.

31. Plato, Republic, bk. VI–VII.

32. Aristotle, Physics.

33. Plato, Cratylus.

34. Aristotle, Metaphysics.

35. Daniel C. Dennett, in "Quining Qualia," from Consciousness Ex-

plained (Boston: Little, Brown and Company, 1991), 368– 94, eliminates qualia as illusory or inconsistent intuitions, arguing they lack explanatory power in scientific accounts. This assumes a representationalist framework; color qualia, as participatory disclosures in light's coherence, align with empirical phenomena like afterimages, preserving their ontological necessity without privacy.

36. Plato, Timaeus.

37. Plato, Republic, bk. VI.

38. Aristotle, Metaphysics.

39. Plato, Cratylus.

40. Aristotle, Physics.

41. Plato, Republic, bk. VII.

42. Robert L. Goldstone and Andrew T. Hendrickson, "Categorical Perception," Wiley Interdisciplinary Reviews: Cognitive Science 1, no. 1 (2010): 69–78, where studies on expertise (e.g., wine sommeliers distinguishing subtle flavors via neural plasticity) show enhanced sensory discrimination. This empirical refinement echoes the artist's participation in disclosed form. Cognitive science supports perceptual attunement through training.

43. Alva Noë, Action in Perception (Cambridge, MA: MIT Press, 2004), which argues perception as skillful activity aligns with vibration's disclosure through participation. Digital art analogies make participation accessible: Pixels as "vibrations" cohere into fractals only through interactive viewing, paralleling how artists engage light's ontology in creation. For related discussions on enactive perception.

44. Goldstone and Hendrickson, "Categorical Perception," Wiley Interdisciplinary Reviews: Cognitive Science 1, no. 1 (2010): 69–78, illustrating perception exceeding hardware limits. This grounds the ontology in adaptive science without reductionism. Hyperacuity in vernier tasks—where practice allows alignment finer than retinal resolution—is exemplified in this book.

45. Aristotle, Metaphysics.

46. Plato, Timaeus.

47. Aristotle, De Anima.

48. Aristotle, Physics; Aristotle, Metaphysics.

49. Francis Bacon, Novum Organum, ed. and trans. Peter Urbach and John Gibson (Chicago: Open Court, 1994); René Descartes, Discourse on Method, trans. Donald A. Cress (Indianapolis: Hackett Publishing Company, 1998).

50. Francis Bacon, Novum Organum.

51. Maurice Merleau-Ponty, Phenomenology of Perception, trans. Donald A. Landes (London: Routledge, 2012).

52. Aristotle, Metaphysics.

53. Aristotle, Physics; Aristotle, Metaphysics.

54. Niklas Luhmann, in Social Systems, translated by John Bednarz Jr. with Dirk Baecker (Stanford, CA: Stanford University Press, 1995), describes modern fragmentation as autopoietic subsystems with binary codes, leading to polycontexturality without overarching unity. This work counters by recovering coherence through vibration's intrinsic disclosure, universal across domains.

55. Aristotle, Poetics, trans. S. H. Butcher, in The Complete Works of Aristotle, vol. 2, ed. Jonathan Barnes (Princeton: Princeton University Press, 1984).

56. Aristotle, Metaphysics.

57. Plato, Republic; Aristotle, Metaphysics.

58. Plato, Timaeus; Aristotle, Metaphysics.

59. Aristotle, Physics; Martin Heidegger, "The Origin of the Work of Art," in Poetry, Language, Thought, trans. Albert Hofstadter (New York: Harper & Row, 1971).

60. Plato, Republic, bk. VI–VII.

61. Plato, Republic, bk. VI–VII; Plato, Timaeus.

62. Plato, Republic, bk. VI; Plato, Timaeus, trans. Donald J. Zeyl (Indianapolis: Hackett Publishing Company, 2000). Supports the claim that metaphysical light names a condition of intelligibility rather than a

physical object.

63. Aristotle, Metaphysics, trans. W. D. Ross, in The Complete Works of Aristotle, vol. 2, ed. Jonathan Barnes (Princeton: Princeton University Press, 1984). Grounds the clarification that levels of articulation do not imply ontological dualism.

64. Aristotle, Physics, trans. R. P. Hardie and R. K. Gaye, in The Complete Works of Aristotle, vol. 1, ed. Jonathan Barnes (Princeton: Princeton University Press, 1984). Supports vibration as processual differentiation rather than brute motion.

65. Plato, Republic, bk. X; Aristotle, Poetics, trans. S. H. Butcher, in The Complete Works of Aristotle, vol. 2, ed. Jonathan Barnes (Princeton: Princeton University Press, 1984). Grounds the claim that art endures because it discloses intelligible structure, not subjective expression.

66. Aristotle, Metaphysics; Martin Heidegger, "The Origin of the Work of Art," in Poetry, Language, Thought, trans. Albert Hofstadter (New York: Harper & Row, 1971). Supports the closing refusal of final explanations and the claim that ontology offers orientation rather than closure.

Bibliography

Aristotle. De Anima. Translated by J. A. Smith. In The Complete Works of Aristotle, Vol. 1, edited by Jonathan Barnes, 641–692. Princeton, NJ: Princeton University Press, 1984.

———. Metaphysics. Translated by W. D. Ross. In The Complete Works of Aristotle, Vol. 2, edited by Jonathan Barnes, 1552–1728. Princeton, NJ: Princeton University Press, 1984.

———. Physics. Translated by R. P. Hardie and R. K. Gaye. In The Complete Works of Aristotle, Vol. 1, edited by Jonathan Barnes, 315–446. Princeton, NJ: Princeton University Press, 1984.

———. Poetics. Translated by S. H. Butcher. In The Complete Works of Aristotle, Vol. 2, edited by Jonathan Barnes, 2316–2340. Princeton, NJ: Princeton University Press, 1984.

Bacon, Francis. Novum Organum. Edited and translated by Peter Urbach and John Gibson. Chicago: Open Court, 1994.

Descartes, René. Discourse on Method. Translated by Donald A. Cress. Indianapolis: Hackett Publishing Company, 1998.

Heidegger, Martin. "The Origin of the Work of Art." In Poetry, Language, Thought, translated by Albert Hofstadter, 15–86. New York: Harper & Row, 1971.

Merleau-Ponty, Maurice. Phenomenology of Perception. Translated by Donald A. Landes. London: Routledge, 2012.

Plato. Cratylus. Translated by C. D. C. Reeve. In Plato: Complete Works, edited by John M. Cooper, 101–156. Indianapolis: Hackett Publishing Company, 1997.

———. Republic. Translated by G. M. A. Grube. Revised by C. D. C. Reeve. Indianapolis: Hackett Publishing Company, 1992.

———. Timaeus. Translated by Donald J. Zeyl. Indianapolis: Hackett Publishing Company, 2000.

Noë, Alva. Action in Perception. Cambridge, MA: MIT Press, 2004.

Thompson, Evan. Mind in Life: Biology, Phenomenology, and the Sciences of Mind. Cambridge, MA: Harvard University Press, 2007.

Varela, Francisco J., Evan Thompson, and Eleanor Rosch. The Embodied Mind. Cambridge, MA: MIT Press, 1991.

Freeman, Walter J. How Brains Make Up Their Minds. New York: Columbia University Press, 1999.

Dennett, Daniel C. "Quining Qualia." In Consciousness Explained, 368–94. Boston: Little, Brown and Company, 1991. (Or reference the original essay in Mind and Cognition, ed. William G. Lycan, 519–35. Oxford: Blackwell, 1990.)

Luhmann, Niklas. Social Systems. Translated by John Bednarz Jr. with Dirk Baecker. Stanford, CA: Stanford University Press, 1995.

Noë, Alva. Action in Perception. Cambridge, MA: MIT Press, 2004.

Saussure, Ferdinand de. Course in General Linguistics. Edited by Charles Bally and Albert Sechehaye. Translated by Wade Baskin. New York: Philosophical Library, 1959.

Goldstone, Robert L., and Andrew T. Hendrickson. "Categorical Perception." Wiley Interdisciplinary Reviews: Cognitive Science 1, no. 1 (2010): 69–78. (For perceptual learning.)

Johann Wolfgang von Goethe, Theory of Colours (Zur Farbenlehre), 1810 (German), 1840 (First English Translation by C.L. Eastlake), Divided into didactic (scientific), polemical (anti-Newtonian), and historical sections, impacted artists like Turner and Kandinsky, and psychologists by focusing on how the eye perceives color, including shadows and complementary colors.

Josef Albers, Interaction of Color, 1963 by Yale University Press, The book serves as a "grammatical lesson" for artists and students, urging them to discover color relationships through play and experimentation rather than passive study.

List of Illustrations

The images included in The Light That Forms function as visual demonstrations rather than decorative figures. They are intended to make perceptible the structural relations discussed in the text— vibration, resonance, geometry, light, and perceptual organization. Unless otherwise noted, illustrations are either public domain, released under Creative Commons licenses, or generated expressly for this work.

Chapter 1

Form Appears from Vibration

Standing Wave Patterns

Visualization of interference and stabilization in oscillatory systems.

Source: Public-domain physics visualizations and educational archives.

Resonance Nodes and Antinodes

Illustration of spatial differentiation produced by vibration.

Source: University physics demonstrations; public domain.

Chapter 2

Sound Becoming Shape

Chladni Plate Patterns

After the experiments of Ernst Chladni (eighteenth century).

Sound-induced geometric forms produced by vibrating surfaces.

Modern reproductions sourced from public-domain and Creative Commons material

Cymatic Sand and Water Patterns

Visible form emerging from acoustic vibration.

After Hans Jenny, Cymatics (1967); contemporary reproductions used for demonstration.

Chapter 3

Geometry Without Design

Natural Symmetry Patterns

Radial and bilateral symmetries arising without design.

Source: Public-domain scientific imagery.

Platonic Solids

Geometric invariants illustrating intelligible form.

After Plato's Timaeus; diagrams adapted from public-domain mathematical sources.

Chapter 4

Light That Is Not Merely Physical

Electromagnetic Spectrum

Diagram situating visible light within the broader physical spectrum.

Source: NASA and other public-domain scientific materials.

Radiant Geometric Structures

Abstract visualization illustrating intelligible order rather than physical illumination.

Source: Generative geometric imagery created for explanatory purposes.

Chapter 5

Vibration as Ontological Process

Harmonic Oscillation Diagrams

Visualization of rhythmic differentiation and coherence.

Source: Public-domain physics and mathematics illustrations.

Standing Waves in Resonant Cavities

Persistence of form through oscillatory process.

Source: Educational physics demonstrations.

Chapter 6

Signs That Mean by Being

Geometric Proportion Diagrams

Illustrations of intrinsic order and proportion.

After Euclid's Elements; public-domain reconstructions.

Chapter 7

Where Is Color?

Color Constancy Demonstrations

Perceptual variation under differing illumination conditions.

Source: Vision science demonstrations, Creative Commons.

Cone Response Curves

Illustration of photoreceptor sensitivity.

Source: Public-domain neuroscience diagrams.

Chapter 8

The Enlightened Artist

Classical Sculpture

Examples of proportional harmony in form.

Source: Public-domain museum photography of Greco-Roman sculpture.

Renaissance Painting and Chiaroscuro

Light as structural disclosure in visual art.

Source: Public-domain works by Renaissance masters.

Chapter 9

Against Fragmentation

Fragmented Knowledge Diagram

Visualization of disciplinary separation.

Source: Contemporary conceptual diagrams, adapted for clarity.

Levels of Organization

Hierarchical coherence across domains.

Source: Systems-theory educational graphics.

Chapter 10

A Classical Ontology for a Fractured Age

Order Emerging from Chaos

Mathematical and physical simulations of spontaneous order.

Source: Public-domain and Creative Commons scientific imagery.

Coherent Oscillatory Fields

Visualization symbolizing integrated intelligibility.

Source: Scientific visualization archives and original renderings.

Note to the Reader

Illustrations in this book are not presented as empirical proofs, but as perceptual demonstrations—aiding the reader in seeing what the argument makes explicit: that form, meaning, and intelligibility are not imposed upon reality, but disclosed through it.

List of Figures and Image Sources

Chapter 1

Form Appears from Vibration

Figure 1.1

Standing wave interference pattern illustrating stabilized vibration.

Source: Public domain physics visualization, Wikimedia Commons.

(Search terms: "standing wave pattern physics")

Figure 1.2

Resonance patterns showing nodal differentiation in oscillatory systems.

Source: Educational physics archive, public domain or Creative Commons.

(Search terms: "wave resonance nodes antinodes")

Chapter 2

Sound Becoming Shape

Figure 2.1

Chladni plate demonstrating sound-induced geometric form.

Source: After experiments by Ernst Chladni, late 18th century.

Modern reproductions available under Creative Commons via Wikimedia Commons.

Figure 2.2

Cymatic sand patterns produced by acoustic vibration.

Source: Experimental documentation inspired by Hans Jenny, Cymatics (1967).

Images available under Creative Commons; original work © Basilius Press.

Chapter 3

Geometry Without Design

Figure 3.1

Radial and bilateral symmetry patterns in natural systems.

Source: Public domain biological and physical pattern archives.

(Search terms: "natural symmetry patterns")

Figure 3.2

Platonic solids illustrating geometric invariance.

Source: Mathematical diagrams derived from Plato, Timaeus.

Modern vector diagrams available under Creative Commons.

Chapter 4

Light That Is Not Merely Physical

Figure 4.1

Electromagnetic spectrum diagram distinguishing visible light from non-visible ranges.

Source: NASA educational materials, public domain.

Figure 4.2

Abstract visualization of radiant geometry used to illustrate intelligible order.

Source: Contemporary generative geometry visualization, Creative Commons.

(Search terms: "radiant geometry abstraction")

Chapter 5

Vibration as Ontological Process

Figure 5.1

Harmonic oscillation diagram showing rhythmic differentiation.

Source: Physics and mathematics educational repositories, public domain.

Figure 5.2

Standing wave in resonant cavity illustrating persistence of form through process.

Source: University physics demonstrations, Creative Commons.

Chapter 6

Signs That Mean by Being

Figure 6.1

Geometric proportion diagram illustrating intrinsic order.

Source: Classical geometry reconstructions after Euclid, Elements.

Public domain.

Chapter 7

Where Is Color?

Figure 7.1

Color perception under varying illumination conditions.

Source: Vision science demonstrations, Creative Commons.

(Search terms: "color constancy illusion")

Figure 7.2

Human retinal cone response curves.

Source: Neuroscience educational materials, public domain.

Chapter 8

The Enlightened Artist

Figure 8.1

Classical sculpture illustrating proportional harmony.

Source: Museum photography of Greco-Roman sculpture, public domain.

Figure 8.2

Renaissance painting demonstrating light as structural disclosure (chiaroscuro).

Source: Public domain artworks (e.g., Caravaggio, Leonardo da Vinci).

Chapter 9

Against Fragmentation

Figure 9.1

Diagram illustrating fragmented disciplinary knowledge.

Source: Contemporary academic visualization, Creative Commons.

Figure 9.2

Hierarchical levels of organization diagram.

Source: Systems theory educational graphics, Creative Commons.

Chapter 10

A Classical Ontology for a Fractured Age

Figure 10.1

Order emerging from chaos visualization.

Source: Mathematical simulation imagery, Creative Commons.

Figure 10.2

Coherent oscillatory field visualization symbolizing integrated intelligibility.

Source: Scientific visualization archive, Creative Commons.

Notes on Image Use

- All images listed are:

    - public domain, or

    - Creative Commons, or

    - reproducible as original diagrams if required by a press

- No copyrighted fine art is required beyond public-domain works

- Images function as philosophical evidence, not illustration

Index